MARKET CONDUCT FOR INVESTMENT MANAGERS

A PRACTICAL GUIDE

David Berman

LATHAM&WATKINS

2019

Published in March 2019
by Thomson Reuters (Professional) UK Limited
Registered in England & Wales, Company No 1679046.
Registered Office and address for service:
5 Canada Square, Canary Wharf, London E14 5AQ

A CIP catalogue record for this book is available from the British Library.

ISBN:9780414071537

Thomson Reuters and the Thomson Reuters logo are trade marks of
Thomson Reuters.
The Latham & Watkins logo is a trade mark of
Latham & Watkins LLP.

Crown copyright material is reproduced with the permission of the Controller of
HMSO and the Queen's Printer for Scotland.

*While all reasonable care has been taken to ensure the accuracy of the publication,
the publishers cannot accept responsibility for any errors or omissions.
This publication is protected by international copyright law.
All rights reserved. No part of this publication may be reproduced or transmitted in any
form or by any means, or stored in any retrieval system of any nature without prior written
permission, except for permitted fair dealing under the Copyright, Designs and Patents
Act 1988, or in accordance with the terms of a licence issued by the Copyright Licensing
Agency in respect of photocopying and/or reprographic reproduction. Application for
permission for other use of copyright material including permission to reproduce extracts
in other published works shall be made to the publishers. Full acknowledgement of
author, publisher and source must be given.*

© 2019 David Berman

CONTENTS

1. Introduction 9
2. Legal and Regulatory Framework 13
3. Fundamental Principles 17
4. Scope and Territoriality of MAR 21
5. Inside Information / MNPI 27
6. Insider Dealing 35
7. Unlawful Disclosure 43
8. Market Manipulation 47
9. Market Soundings 53
10. Loans and Other "Out-of-Scope" Instruments 61
11. Company Meetings / Dialogue 65
12. Einhorn / Greenlight 69
13. Rumours 85
14. Suspicious Transactions and Orders 89
15. Common "Buy-Side" Issues 93
16. Practicalities 97
17 Scenarios 105
Index 115

ACKNOWLEDGEMENTS

I would like to thank the very many investment professionals whose paths I have crossed over recent years – for their practical insights and inspiration to put pen to paper. I am equally grateful to the various in-house Legal and Compliance teams for their on-going loyalty, tricky technical questions(!) and encouragement.

Many thanks also to my esteemed fellow partners, Rob Moulton, Nicola Higgs, Andrea Monks and Carl Fernandes, for providing invaluable input and challenge.

Last but not least, a huge "thank you" to my family (Debbie, Aaron, Eva and Georgia) for their unswerving support and remarkable patience.

David Berman, 2019

PREFACE

Market conduct is, and will almost certainly remain, an area of concerted regulatory focus. Market abuse risk is also arguably the single greatest risk faced by investment managers on a day-to-day basis.

Many texts have been published into the generalities and technicalities of the market conduct regime. However, none (to date at least) has focused on the so-called "buy-side". This guide is therefore the first of its kind – not only in terms of its particular focus, but also its decidedly practical approach.

Buy-side investment professionals face a distinct range of market conduct issues – some more commonly-occurring than others; and which are often far from straightforward. This publication is intended as a practical "one-stop" reference guide for investment managers. While it does not profess to have all of the answers to all scenarios (an impossible feat!), this guide is designed to help investment professionals to navigate this important, and complex, area – by raising levels of awareness and intuitive understanding. This is achieved through (amongst other things) the medium of real-world insights and a host of case studies and practical scenarios.

David Berman, 2019

GUEST FOREWORD

David Berman has written a timely and apposite book for all buy-side investment, compliance and legal professionals.

"Market" and "Conduct" are both dynamic concepts in our economy as we adapt our thinking to the opportunities of volatility and ambiguity. David provides a clear and instructive guide through the key issues and questions that practitioners face as they invest their clients' funds across private and public forums to meet their needs and expectations. In doing so, investment firms need to balance the individual and common good in a just and fair way, recognising the global and immediate interconnectedness of market participants, users and beneficiaries. This book is a very practical guide to the issues to which this gives rise.

David's experience in the industry as well as his approach as a hands-on adviser makes him particularly well-placed to help his clients answer the question: "Thanks for telling us the law: what do we need to do in practice?"

Howard Trust
General Counsel at Schroders

GLOSSARY OF ABBREVIATIONS / DEFINITIONS

AIMA – Alternative Investment Management Association

BCI – Borrower Confidential Information

DMP – disclosing market participant

ESMA – European Securities and Markets Authority

FCA – Financial Conduct Authority

FSA – Financial Services Authority

IPO – initial public offering

LMA – Loan Market Association

LOOI – Loans and other 'out-of-scope' instruments

MAR – Market Abuse Regulation

MSR – market sounding recipient

MTF – multilateral trading facility

NDA – non-disclosure agreement

OTF – organised trading facility

RTS – Regulatory Technical Standards

SCI – Syndicate Confidential Information

STORs – suspicious transactions and order reports

1
INTRODUCTION

Backdrop

Market conduct risk is arguably the single most significant form of day-to-day risk faced by asset managers. As many market participants would testify, certain key aspects of the UK/EU market conduct regime can be very difficult to navigate and apply in practice. This issue can be attributed to a combination of: (a) the inherent (albeit unavoidable) "greyness" of certain core concepts (such as the constituent elements of the definition of "inside information"); and (b) the highly fact-sensitive nature of the regime, where no two scenarios are ever identical.

With potentially severe and franchise-threatening / career-limiting consequences for crossing the line – even "innocent" inadvertent breaches – market practitioners must tread carefully. In an ideal world, the legislators would have laid down a set of bright "red lines", which could be readily applied to any particular fact-pattern. However, that is impossible to achieve – given the infinite number of scenarios that can arise in practice.

Instead, market conduct is regulated through a set of high-level core concepts / definitions, supplemented by explanatory provisions (recitals) and technical standards or guidelines relating to specific areas of the regime. While this internationally common construct has the benefit of broad coverage, it has the corresponding drawback of being vague in various important respects.

Objective

Numerous books have been published on the technical detail of the market conduct regime; and we do not seek to add to that body of literature. Rather, **this publication seeks to provide an intuitive and**

Introduction

illuminative guide through the technicalities to deliver practical solutions for "buy-side" investment professionals and control functions. It is intended to serve as a user-friendly point of reference for tricky market conduct conundrums, with which investment managers are faced on a frequent basis. Questions addressed include (amongst many others):

- Are we "inside"?
- Can we legitimately consider this information to be in the public domain?
- How should we apply the "reasonable investor test" in practice?
- Can we now consider ourselves "cleansed"?
- How should we respond to an inadvertent wall-crossing?
- How do we manage the risks inherent within company meetings / dialogue?
- In what circumstances can we legitimately use "big-boy" letters?
- To what extent can we rely upon the assurances provided to us by a third party (for instance, that information is not "inside information")?
- Is this scenario actually a "market-sounding"?
- Is it ever possible, in reality, for us to rebut the presumption that, if we trade while in possession of inside information, we have "used" that information (and therefore insider dealt)?

This guide draws upon years of front-line experience and insight; and includes a host of "buy-side"- focused scenarios, case studies and "war stories" – designed to "bring issues to life".

No right-thinking investment professional would ever wish to be the subject of a regulatory investigation, which can run for many months, if not years. Such investigations are deeply unsettling and all-consuming – even if they happen to result in no eventual sanction. This publication is designed to help investment professionals to understand: (i) the boundaries of the relevant offences (i.e. where the illegitimate edge lies); and (ii) how to avoid going too near to that edge (by not providing the regulator with any reason to open an investigation in the first place).

Practical pointers are highlighted throughout in blue text.

Introduction

Focus of coverage

This publication focuses predominantly on the *civil* UK/EU market abuse regime (the Market Abuse Regulation (MAR)[1] – given that the significant majority of markets-related regulatory enforcement activity tends to be brought under the civil, rather than criminal, regime. Clearly, this does not mean that the criminal regime can (or should) be effectively disregarded[2] – rather, that it was considered most prudent (and practically useful) to focus on the civil regime, with its lower evidential burdens and thresholds, and broader scope. In turn, this has helped to keep the length of this book down to a hopefully digestible minimum!

Organisational level considerations – such as systems and controls

Organisational level requirements – such as market conduct systems and controls and surveillance – are outside the scope of this guide.

Brexit

From a UK perspective, it is not anticipated that the key themes and principles discussed in this book would be materially impacted on account of Brexit.

Target audience

This guide is **aimed at "buy-side" investment managers**; and **assumes a base knowledge of the core aspects of the UK/EU market regime**. It is intended to be equally useful and instructive for **both front line investment professionals and second line control functions**.

---

[1] As implemented in the UK; and as interpreted by the UK courts.
[2] Not least, because the Regulators can, and increasingly do, bring criminal prosecutions for market misconduct.

Introduction

Terminology

The terms "asset manager", "investment manager", "fund manager" "buy-side firm" and "buy-side institution" are used interchangeably throughout this publication.

Outline

Chapter 2 outlines the applicable legal and regulatory framework; with chapter 3 drawing out the important underpinning principles of the regime; and chapter 4 covering the scope and territorial reach of MAR.

Chapter 5 explains the notion of inside information; which is central to the offences of insider dealing (chapter 6) and unlawful disclosure (chapter 7). Chapter 8 briefly summarises the various market manipulation offences.

Market soundings are covered in chapter 9; while loans and other "out-of-scope" instruments are discussed in chapter 10.

Company meetings / dialogue and the seminal *Einhorn / Greenlight* case are discussed in chapter, 11 and 12, respectively.

Chapter 13 focuses on rumours; with suspicious transactions and orders addressed in chapter 14.

Common "buy-side" issues and are highlighted in chapter 15.

Chapter 16 includes a host of practical pointers / issues to consider. Finally, various "real-life" scenarios are discussed in chapter 17.

Important Notice

While it is hoped that this publication serves as a helpful practical guide, its contents do not constitute, and cannot therefore be relied upon as, legal advice. Every situation will turn on its own factual matrix; accordingly, professional advice should be sought in specific cases.

2
LEGAL AND REGULATORY FRAMEWORK

Criminal regime

Many jurisdictions, including the UK, operate a criminal securities regime alongside a civil regime. In broad terms, the criminal and civil regimes overlap significantly – in terms of the general types of behaviours that are outlawed. For instance, in the UK, it is a criminal offence for a person who has information as an "insider" to deal in price-affected securities in relation to that information[3]. Under the civil market abuse regime, as we will subsequently explore in further detail, a person who uses "inside information" in relation to a particular security to deal in that security (or a derivative thereof) is guilty of the offence of "insider dealing".

There are similarly comparable criminal and civil offences relating to the improper or unlawful disclosure of "inside information"; and to certain forms of "market manipulation".

However, notwithstanding the apparent similarities and overlap, there are also some important differences between the criminal and civil regimes – most obviously, relating to: the respective standards of proof[4] (and associated evidential burden); the generally more restrictive circumstances in which the criminal regime can be invoked; the mental intent required by the criminal regime; and the availability of various specific defences under the criminal regime.

A detailed exposition of the criminal securities regime is beyond the scope of this publication. That should not, however, be taken to suggest that the criminal regime can be effectively ignored in practice

---

[3] Section 53(1) Criminal Justice Act 1993.
[4] Criminal – beyond reasonable doubt; civil – balance of probabilities.

– the regulatory authorities can, and do, bring successful criminal prosecutions.

Sanctions under the criminal regime include: imprisonment for up to seven years; fines; public censure; and prohibitions.

Civil regime

The significant majority of securities-related cases are brought under the *civil* regime – which is not especially surprising, given the lower standard of proof and broader (easier-to-satisfy) constituent element definitions or tests. Civil cases also tend to be far less costly and time-consuming for the regulatory authorities. On that basis, it was considered most prudent (and practically useful) for this publication to focus on the civil regime – which might be regarded as the "lowest common denominator" for practical purposes.

Market Abuse Regulation (MAR)

MAR is the primary source of civil market conduct regulation.

Sanctions for breach of MAR include one or more of: unlimited fines; public censure; and prohibitions.

As is customary for European regulations, MAR begins with a host of (often overlooked) explanatory recitals (**Recitals**). In essence, these Recitals are intended to provide supplementary colour to the core articles; and to articulate underlying legislative intent – serving as helpful contextualisation and backdrop. This is particularly significant in the context of a regime which, by its very nature, cannot possibly legislate for every real-life scenario.

Therefore, where (as will often be the case) a given fact-pattern does not neatly align with the specific provisions of MAR, it will be necessary to apply a "back to fundamental principles" analysis – consistent with the **requisite *purposive* interpretation of MAR**. As will become apparent, the Recitals can prove to be invaluable in such instances.

Legal and regulatory framework

Regulatory Technical Standards (RTS), Guidelines, and Q&A

MAR is supplemented with a number of ancillary (and topic-specific) provisions contained, variously, in the form of RTS, Guidelines and Q&A (as updated from time to time)[5].

For example, there is a set of RTS[6] in relation to the appropriate arrangements, systems and procedures for disclosing market participants (DMPs) conducting market soundings. Similarly, there are corresponding Guidelines[7] for recipients of such market soundings.

Further, a continually evolving Q&A[8] document, answers specific MAR-related questions that have been raised with the European Securities and Markets Authority (ESMA).

As a practical matter, these documents should also be consulted when considering any specific MAR-related scenario. Additionally, it would be prudent to check for any FCA (Financial Conduct Authority) final notices or tribunal decisions that may be "on-point" or analogous to the situation at hand.

FCA Principles

All UK-regulated financial institutions are subject to a set of high-level principles, the breach of which can alone form the basis of a regulatory enforcement action. Indeed, the majority of enforcement cases against firms have been founded on a contravention of such principles (as opposed to technical underlying rules).

In addition to the need to act with integrity, firms must also (amongst other things) "observe proper standards of market conduct". Approved persons[9] or in-scope individuals[10] must observe identical conduct rules, failing which they would be exposed to personal enforcement action.

---

[5] For completeness, it is also supplemented with a Delegated Regulation and an Implementing Directive.
[6] https://eur-lex.europa.eu/legal-content/EN/TXT/PDF/?uri=CELEX:32016R0960&from=EN.
[7] https://www.esma.europa.eu/sites/default/files/library/2016-1477_mar_guidelines_-_market_soundings.pdf.
[8] https://www.esma.europa.eu/sites/default/files/library/esma70-145-111_qa_on_mar.pdf.
[9] Under the Approved Persons Regime.
[10] As defined under the Senior Managers & Certification Regime.

Legal and regulatory framework

Sanctions include one or more of: unlimited fines, public censures and prohibitions.

Significantly, the ambit of the "proper market conduct standards" principle is not confined to the scope of MAR. By way of example, an unauthorised disclosure of sensitive information relating to a technically out-of-MAR-scope security could still be viewed as a failure to observe proper standards of market conduct – notwithstanding that, on technical grounds, it may fall outside the ambit of MAR. Indeed, this is precisely what happened in the case of *Nicholas Kyprios*[11], who was fined £210,000 and publicly censured for his misdeeds.

The high-level nature of the "proper market conduct standards" principle; and its potentially broad application, thus provides the Regulator with an alternative enforcement channel.

The fundamental principles discussed in the next chapter[12] (the **"Fundamental Principles"**) can serve as a useful proxy for the interpretation of "proper standards of market conduct". As a general working rule of thumb, where a proposed course of conduct could be perceived as offending against the Fundamental Principles, it might prudently be assumed that such a scenario will attract regulatory interest and scrutiny – **irrespective of whether or not it technically falls within the scope of MAR**. It would therefore be unwise to seek to rely on purely technical arguments to justify or excuse behaviour that would **nevertheless** likely be regarded as offending against the Fundamental Principles – to which we now turn.

---

[11] http://www.fsa.gov.uk/static/pubs/final/nicholas-kyprios.pdf
[12] Which essentially underpin the MAR regime.

3

FUNDAMENTAL PRINCIPLES

Before discussing the various market abuse offences, it is first instructive to stand back and consider the Fundamental Principles underlying the market conduct regime.

Unfair advantage obtained from the (mis-)use of "inside information"[13]

Relevant extracts from Recitals (23) and (24) of MAR are replicated below, respectively [our emphasis]:

*"The essential characteristic of insider dealing consists in an **unfair advantage** being **obtained from inside information** to the **detriment of third parties who are unaware of such information** and, consequently, the undermining of the integrity of financial markets and investor confidence. Consequently, the prohibition against insider dealing should apply **where a person who is in possession of inside information takes unfair advantage of** the benefit gained from that information **by entering into market transactions** in accordance with that **information** by acquiring or disposing of, by attempting to acquire or dispose of, by cancelling or amending, or by attempting to cancel or amend, an order to acquire or dispose of, for his own account or for the account of a third party, directly or indirectly, financial instruments to which that information relates."*

"Where a legal or natural person in possession of inside information acquires or disposes of, or attempts to acquire or dispose of, for his own account or for the account of a third party, directly or indirectly, financial instruments to which that information relates, it should be implied that that person has used that information. That presumption is without prejudice to the rights of the defence. ***The question whether a person***

---

[13] As discussed in chapters 5 and 6 below.

has infringed the prohibition on insider dealing or has attempted to commit insider dealing should be analysed in the light of the **purpose of this Regulation**, *which is to protect the integrity of the financial market and to enhance investor confidence, which is based, in turn, on* **the assurance that investors will be placed on an equal footing and** *protected from the misuse of inside information.*"

The following Fundamental Principles can be gleaned from these extracts:

- The "insider dealing"[14] offence is concerned with the mis-use of the content / import of inside information …
- Which thereby results in an unfair advantage being gained (by the user) to the corresponding detriment of unknowing third parties.
- A person who deals whilst in possession of inside information is rebuttably presumed to have "insider dealt".
- MAR is to be interpreted purposively.
- Investors are presumed to operate on a level informational playing-field.

Accurate impression of price, supply and demand

The various "market manipulation" offences[15] are broadly underpinned by the Fundamental Principles that:

- at any given time, the market (and its participants) has an accurate and not misleading impression of the price or supply of, or demand for, a particular financial instrument (or a related derivative);
- prices are not improperly secured at artificial levels; and
- demand is not improperly squeezed.

Practical application

As explained in the previous chapter, it will often be the case that a given fact-pattern does not neatly fit within the specific provisions of MAR. In such circumstances, it is often instructive to consider

---

[14] Discussed more fully in chapter 6 below.
[15] Summarised in chapter 8 below.

whether the situation at hand offends against any of the Fundamental Principles.

As a general rule of thumb, if the scenario does not – from any angle – offend against the Fundamental Principles, then it is likely to be acceptable, from a MAR perspective. Put another way, and adopting the requisite purposive interpretation of MAR, it is of itself unlikely to be of interest to a regulator.

Conversely, where a particular set of circumstances does (or may) offend against the Fundamental Principles, that should be regarded as a "red flag"; and, without more, assumed to be inappropriate. In other words, it would be prudent to assume that such conduct will be viewed dimly by a regulator.

4
SCOPE AND TERRITORIALITY OF MAR

Scope of MAR

This section summarises the most likely relevant provisions; and should not be treated as an exhaustive exposition. MAR applies to "financial instruments":

(a) Admitted to trading on an EU-regulated market or for which a request for admission to trading on a regulated market has been made.

(b) Traded on an EU multilateral trading facility (MTF), admitted to trading on an EU MTF or for which a request for admission to trading on an EU MTF has been made;

(c) Traded on an EU organised trading facility (OTF).

(d) Not covered by points (a), (b) or (c), the price or value of which depends or has an effect on the price or value of a financial instrument referred to in those points, including, but not limited to, credit default swaps and contracts for difference.

Irrespective of whether or not the relevant transaction, order or conduct concerning the financial instrument takes place on a trading venue.

MAR also applies to **both** natural and legal persons.

Key definitions

"Financial instruments" include:

- Transferrable securities – those classes of securities which are negotiable on the capital market, with the exception of instruments of payment, such as: (a) shares in companies and other securities equivalent to shares in companies, partnerships or other entities, and depositary receipts in respect of shares; (b) bonds or other forms of securitised debt, including depositary receipts in respect of such securities; and (c) any other securities giving the right to acquire or sell any such transferable securities or giving rise to a cash settlement determined by reference to transferable securities, currencies, interest rates or yields, commodities or other indices or measures.
- Money-market instruments – those classes of instruments which are normally dealt in on the money market, such as treasury bills, certificates of deposit and commercial papers, excluding instruments of payment.
- Units in collective investment undertakings.
- Options, futures, swaps, forward rate agreements and any other derivative contracts relating to securities, currencies, interest rates or yields, emission allowances or other derivative instruments, financial indices or financial measures which may be settled physically or in cash.
- Options, futures, swaps, forwards and any other derivative contracts relating to commodities that must be settled in cash or may be settled in cash at the option of one of the parties other than by reason of default or other termination event.
- Options, futures, swaps, and any other derivative contract relating to commodities that can be physically settled provided that they are traded on a regulated market, a MTF, or an OTF, except for wholesale energy products traded on an OTF that must be physically settled.
- Options, futures, swaps, forwards and any other derivative contracts relating to commodities, that can be physically settled not otherwise mentioned in the above bullet and not being for

commercial purposes, which have the characteristics of other derivative financial instruments.
- Derivative instruments for the transfer of credit risk.
- Financial contracts for difference.

"Regulated market": a multilateral system operated and/or managed by a market operator, which brings together or facilitates the bringing together of multiple third-party buying and selling interests in financial instruments – in the system and in accordance with its non-discretionary rules – in a way that results in a contract, in respect of the financial instruments admitted to trading under its rules and/or systems, and which is authorised and functions regularly.

"MTF": a multilateral system, operated by an investment firm or a market operator, which brings together multiple third-party buying and selling interests in financial instruments – in the system and in accordance with non-discretionary rules – in a way that results in a contract.

"OTF": a multilateral system which is not a regulated market or an MTF and in which multiple third-party buying and selling interests in bonds, structured finance products, emission allowances or derivatives are able to interact in the system in a way that results in a contract.

"Trading venue": a regulated market, MTF or OTF.

Territorial application of MAR

The prohibitions and requirements in MAR apply to actions and omissions, in the EU **and in a third country**, concerning in-scope financial instruments.

The geographical scope of MAR is limited only by MAR's application to instruments which are listed, or traded/tradeable on EU venues. In other words, the country of incorporation relevant to the instrument, the location of the people involved in (for example) handling inside information, and the location of the investors, are not decisive. Article 2(4) of MAR clarifies that the regime applies to "actions and omissions in the Union and in a third country".

Accordingly, a third country-based investor who insider deals in relation to an in-scope financial instrument is subject to MAR sanction. The extra-territorial reach of the market conduct regime (effectively, now MAR) was neatly illustrated in the well-publicised *Einhorn / Greenlight* case[16], in which David Einhorn, the owner of Greenlight, was found[17] to have insider traded in relation to a UK-listed stock (Punch Taverns Plc) – notwithstanding that all relevant trading activity was conducted out of the US and that Einhorn / Greenlight had no UK/EU presence.

Instruments whose price or value depends on or has an effect on a MAR financial instrument

MAR applies not only to financial instruments listed or traded/tradeable on EU venues, but also to other instruments the price or value of which depends or has an effect on the price or value of such an instrument. There is some uncertainty over how broadly this should be interpreted. The examples provided in the legislation are relatively narrow – credit default swaps and contracts for difference are explicitly cited; and ESMA has subsequently pronounced that a similar link will be expected between shares of a parent and its subsidiary. However, in each case, these are pretty close proxies for the instrument itself. For example, a contract for difference will give a direct and potentially leveraged exposure to changes in the value of the financial instrument.

However, what about an index? If a person was inside on a company in the FTSE 100, arguably significant changes in the share price of that company would have a small impact on the price or value of the FTSE. Or if a fund had a significant investment in a particular company, would being inside on that company also make the same person inside on the fund? These circumstances will be highly fact-specific. It would be prudent to assume that, if the instrument is an objectively reasonable proxy for a MAR in-scope instrument, it is probably also caught. Conversely, it is unlikely that MAR was intended to prevent someone that is inside on a single constituent of a large and broad index to be unable to trade in that index to, for example, hedge other risks.

A further illustrative example is provided in the following chapter.

---

[16] 2012.
[17] Along with Greenlight itself; each were fined in excess of £3.5 million.

Practicalities

The ambit, coverage and territorial application of MAR are extremely broad. In practice, therefore, investment professionals might prudently assume that, one way or another (and to some degree, at least), their day-to-day activities will fall within scope.

Further, it would be unwise to seek to rely on purely technical arguments to justify or excuse behaviour that, **even if** technically out of MAR's scope, would **nevertheless** likely be regarded as offending against the Fundamental Principles.

Current regulatory expectations

The following extract from an FCA speech[18] highlights the increased regulatory focus on (amongst other things) non-equity asset classes [our emphasis]:

*"… the prevention of market abuse is a **multi-asset exercise**, and therefore, by definition a complex one. Equity insider dealing has been a clear focus in the past, which is reflected by many of our outcomes to date being focused on that behaviour. However, **all relevant markets** are vulnerable to both insider dealing and manipulation, therefore we are now even more focused on seeking out evidence of market manipulation across asset classes and combatting abuse wherever we find it.*

London is a critical global trading centre across the asset classes and our pursuit of secondary market abuse must reflect the scope of our markets; and it does.

If compliance with the market abuse regime is a state of mind, then the state of mind that market abuse only takes place in equities, which still feels like an unreconstructed assumption in certain areas of the market, needs to be thoroughly broken."

Therefore, the fact that the majority of published market abuse cases to date have related to the equity markets, should **not** be taken as indicating a lack of regulatory interest in other asset classes.

---

[18] Speech by Julia Hoggett, FCA Director of Market Oversight, November 2017.

5

INSIDE INFORMATION / MNPI

Contextual backdrop

As discussed further in the following chapter, the concept of "inside information" (often colloquially referred to as "MNPI") is integral to the "insider dealing" offence[19]; which is the single most relevant form of market abuse for the "buy-side".

It is therefore essential that investment professionals are familiar with the definition of "inside information".

"Inside Information" – defined

Inside information comprises information of a *precise nature*, which has *not been made public*, relating directly or indirectly, to one or more issuers or to one or more financial instruments, and which, if it were made public, would be *likely to have a significant effect on the prices* of those financial instruments or on the price of related derivative financial instruments.[20]

Therefore, in order for information to be classed as "inside information" (for the purposes of MAR), it must satisfy **each** of the following elements:

(1) Precise nature

For these purposes, information shall be deemed to be of a precise nature if:

---

[19] And also the "unlawful disclosure" offence – covered in chapter 7 below.
[20] Article 7.1(a) of MAR.

(a) it indicates a set of circumstances which exists or which *may reasonably be expected* to come into existence, or an event which has occurred or which *may reasonably be expected* to occur; and

(b) where it is specific enough to enable a conclusion to be drawn as to the *possible effect* of that set of circumstances or event on the prices of the financial instruments or the related derivative financial instruments.[21]

In this context, "may reasonably be expected" means "there is a realistic prospect that". This is a low bar; and significantly lower than the "more likely than not" interpretation historically utilised by certain market participants. An event may therefore be reasonably expected to occur even if the chances are that it will not occur. With the bar thus set (low and unspecific), market participants will invariably face difficulties in its practical application. According to one rule of thumb, if a deal has legs, and bankers/lawyers, etc. working on it, then they are unlikely to be wasting their time on a deal which is unlikely to occur. However, if a potential transaction is being contemplated by one party, but has not been discussed with the other party, it would not ordinarily be reasonably expected to occur.

In determining "possible effect", it is *not* necessary to be able to draw a conclusion as to the possible *direction* of any share price movement.[22]

(2) Non-public

In many cases, it is readily apparent that information is in the public domain. However, in other situations this question may be less clear-cut. Each individual scenario must be assessed on its particular facts in order to determine whether it can legitimately be deemed public.

The following factors are indications that information has been made public – whether:

- the information has been disclosed via a regulatory information service;

---

[21] Article 7.2 of MAR.
[22] *Lafonta v AMF* (C-628/13).

- the information is contained in records which are open to public inspection;
- the information is otherwise generally available, including through the Internet, or some other publication (including if it is only available on payment of a fee), or is derived from public information; and
- the information can be obtained by observation by members of the public without infringing rights or obligations of privacy, property or confidentiality.

Illustrative example

The FCA provides an illustrative example[23]. If a passenger on a train passing a burning factory calls his broker and tells him to sell shares in the factory's owner, the passenger will be using information which has been made public – since it is information obtained by legitimate means through observation of a public event.

Another example would involve the use of survey data. If a party commissions a survey, the information obtained by that survey might be price-sensitive (for example, it could compare the customers' satisfaction levels at competitors, or relate to a political event such as the Brexit referendum). However, on the basis that any person could have commissioned the survey, the information is considered to be public, even though in practice it is only known by one person because only that person commissioned the survey.

However, the position may well be different if, for example, the person commissioning the survey attempted to prevent other people from mandating a similar survey through an exclusivity arrangement. In these circumstances, such information could potentially be regarded as non-public information.

Case study

A portfolio manager (PM) attends an investee company meeting, alongside seven portfolio managers from other institutions. The

---

[23] MAR1.1.14G.

company's CFO inadvertently discloses some inside information at the meeting.

Can PM legitimately consider herself not to possess inside information – on the basis that the seven other attendees have also been made privy to that information; and, therefore, that she can legitimately conclude that it is "public"?

In a word, no – that would be an extremely bold conclusion to draw and one that, without more, would be unlikely to elicit much regulatory sympathy, if challenged. Unfortunately (albeit perhaps understandably), there is no "magic number" at or beyond which information can readily be assumed to be "public". Obviously, the larger the number, the easier it should be to reach such a conclusion. For instance, if this was a large conference, attended by say 1,000 attendees or a conference call with several hundred participants. However, as always, this must be a case-by-case determination – as every situation is so highly fact-specific.

As a practical matter, where there is some doubt over whether information has been made public (in this context), and the information is ultimately adjudged to be in the public domain, it is always prudent to maintain a record of the basis upon which such a conclusion was reached; together, wherever possible, with supporting contemporaneous evidence (such as screen-shot print-offs, analyst reports, external counsel advice, etc.).

(3) Likely to have a significant price effect

"Likely" in this context means: "there is a real prospect that".

"Significant effect on prices" means: "information a reasonable investor would be likely to use as part of the basis of his or her investment decisions"[24].

This "reasonable investor" test can be difficult to apply in practice, given its inherent vagueness. MAR does, however, provide some guidance [our emphasis]:

---

[24] Article 7.4 of MAR.

"Reasonable investors base their investment decisions on information already available to them ... Therefore, the question whether, in making an investment decision, a reasonable investor would be likely to take into account a particular piece of information should be analysed on the basis of ex ante available information. **Such an assessment has to take into consideration: (i) the anticipated impact of the information in light of the totality of the related issuer's activities; (ii) the reliability of the source of the information; and (iii) any other market variables likely to affect the financial instruments ... in the given circumstances.**"[25]

It is relatively common in practice for firms to use an appropriate[26] seasoned in-house investment professional as an effective proxy for the "reasonable investor"; and (often on a "no-names" basis) to solicit their views on a particular situation. Indeed, there is arguably no obviously better way in which to try and determine the mind-set of the "reasonable investor".

In any event, the ultimate assessment should be documented (including underlying reasoning) and placed on file.

Case study

A fund manager, FM, runs a fund which is invested in a listed investment trust (L). L holds numerous investee company stocks within its portfolio "basket". Following a market-sounding, FM has positive inside information in respect of one of the investee company stocks (Z) (which constitutes 2% of the overall basket).

FM wishes to acquire some more L shares. Is FM inside on L, on account of her possession of inside information regarding Z?

Given the composition of the basket – with Z representing only 2% of the overall basket – FM would not be inside on L; and is therefore free to follow through with her purchase.

As a general rule of thumb, the higher the percentage represented by Z of the overall basket, the more likely that FM might also be regarded as inside on L. Unfortunately, there is no clear numeric threshold, beyond

---

[25] Recital (14) of MAR.
[26] Typically, with expertise and experience in the particular market / instruments concerned.

Inside information / MNPI

which FM would be inside on L; and below which she would not. That said, it should be relatively easy to conclude that a percentage (for Z) of less than 10% of the overall basket did not – without more – amount to inside information in relation to L.

As always, this will be a highly fact-specific analysis, based on the totality of the facts and circumstances.

Intermediate steps

An intermediate step in a protracted process shall be deemed to be "inside information" if, by itself, it satisfies the criteria of "inside information".

Rounded assessment

Any inside information determination should be made: (i) against the entirety of available facts; and (ii) in the context in which the information is disclosed / received. As, for example, with the *Einhorn / Greenlight* case, context can be critically important.

Source / origin of inside information

Importantly, inside information need not have originated from the issuer to which the information relates. For instance, an unpublished note from an influential research analyst which contains a change of recommendation could, in and of itself, constitute inside information (on the subject company).

Similarly, knowledge of a recently (or imminently to be) placed significant (i.e. potentially market-moving) order is likely to amount to inside information.[27]

"Read-across" scenarios

Issuers

It is possible[28] that, in certain circumstances, inside information relating to one company (A) may *also* constitute inside information in

---

[27] See further the "front-running" example cited in the following chapter.
[28] Albeit, this will be more the exception, rather than the norm.

relation to another company (B). This will always be a very fact-specific determination; and will likely depend upon a number of factors, including (but not limited to):

- The nature / import of the inside information itself – for example, whether it is very specific to Company A and therefore unlikely to have any material implications for company B / the wider sector.
- Whether A and B operate in the same industry / sector; and share similar characteristics (e.g. customer-base, products, technologies, locations, regulatory environments, financial conditions, etc.), which, in the circumstances, increase the likelihood of Company B also being affected by the inside information.
- If so, the number of other listed issuers within the same industry / sector.
- The relative significance of Company A in the context of the wider listed sector / industry as a whole. For instance, is Company A a relative minnow?

Financial instruments

In a similar vein, where an issuer has more than one type of in-MAR-scope financial instrument – for example, listed equity and listed bonds – it will always be necessary to consider whether inside information held in relation to one (say, here, the equity) also constitutes inside information on the other (here, the bonds). While, in many cases one will indeed impact the other, this does not automatically follow; and should always be assessed on a case-by-case basis.

The importance of ongoing awareness and sound judgement

The difficulty in applying the "inside information" definition in practice has been acknowledged by the regulator[29] [our emphasis]:

*"I'll start with the definition of inside information – something which is central to the market abuse regime – **its very definition is both fluid and situational**. The information must be of a precise nature, not have been made public, relate directly or indirectly to one or more issuers or*

---

[29] Speech by Julia Hoggett, FCA Director of Market Oversight, November 2017.

financial instruments and fundamentally, if made public, be likely to have a significant effect on the prices of those financial instruments or related derivatives.

Even applying that statement in practice requires a set of **situational judgements** to be made by relevant parties across the industry (and indeed those who might not even consider themselves to be in the industry at all). Defining inside information cannot be just a set of rules, therefore, it must be a state of mind, a vigilance to identify the potential for such information and the skill to have the capacity to make the assessment as to whether the conditions are met and then, simply put, the awareness of what to do next. There is a risk therefore that systems and controls will only go so far if that critical thinking has not taken place."

The theme of high vigilance features heavily in the following chapter, "Insider Dealing".

6

INSIDER DEALING

Insider dealing is arguably the single most relevant market abuse offence, from the perspective of a buy-side institution / investment professional.

The offence

Insider dealing arises[30] where a [legal or natural] person possesses inside information (as defined in the previous chapter) and *uses* that information by transacting, for its own account or for that of another, directly or indirectly, financial instruments to which that information relates.

The *use of* inside information by cancelling or amending an order concerning a financial instrument to which the information relates, where the order was placed before the person possessed the inside information, shall also be considered to be insider dealing.[31]

Attempting

An attempt to engage in insider dealing is, in and of itself, an offence.

Inducing and recommending

The recommending or inducing of another person, by an insider and on the basis of inside information, to engage in insider dealing, is also an offence[32].

---

[30] Under Article 8.1 of MAR.
[31] Article 8.1 of MAR.
[32] Articles 8(2) and 14(b) of MAR.

Rebuttable presumption

A person possessing inside information who transacts in financial instruments to which that information relates will be presumed to have "used" that information; and therefore to have insider dealt. This presumption can be rebutted if it can be established that the inside information was not in fact "used" when carrying out the transaction[33] – in other words, if it can be shown that the inside information did not in fact influence the transaction decision.

Where it is proposed to rely upon a rebuttal of this presumption, it would be prudent to document the underlying reasoning, ideally supported with contemporaneous evidence, where available. For instance, if a particular investment decision was made **prior to** the receipt of inside information in relation to the stock concerned, evidence of that decision, its rationale(s) and timing should be kept on file. If ever necessary, this should serve to prove that the inside information could not possibly have been "used" to influence the investment decision, as that decision had already been taken by the time that inside information entered the organisation.

Scope

Significantly, the "insider dealing" offence and its variants outlined above, will extend to persons who: (a) know; **or (b) ought to know** that it is inside information. When considering whether a person (P) ought to have known that information was inside, the regulators will consider what a "normal and reasonable" person in the position of P should have known in the circumstances.[34]

Limb (b) is an especially significant provision for buy-side institutions and investment professionals. In essence, it is irrelevant whether a person actually appreciated that they were in possession of inside information[35] – if they, **nevertheless, *ought to have realised* as much**. It is important (if not somewhat sobering) to consider the relative ease with which the regulator can allege that an investment professional

---

[33] Recitals (24) and (25) of MAR.
[34] Recital (26) of MAR.
[35] MAR 1.2.9G.

simply ought to have realised that they possessed inside information. In other words, **ignorance will not constitute a defence**.

The insider dealing case brought against David Einhorn and his Greenlight fund provides a neat example of the practical application of this provision. A key plank of Einhorn's / Greenlight's defence was that he / it did not actually realise that they had received inside information. Whether this was or was not in fact the case did not matter, as the regulator simply asserted that they **ought to have known** that they were "inside". And that was essentially enough – there was nowhere left for the defendants to turn.

Ongoing vigilance and awareness

Against this backdrop, it is vital that investment professionals maintain a high state of vigilance and awareness – especially, when interacting with issuers or their advisers, or with others who are known or suspected to be "insiders".

"If firms receive inside information but it is not identified as such, there is a significant risk that this information is acted on in breach of market abuse rules. Firms should consider the benefit relative to the risk of attending meetings where there is a significant possibility that inside information might be inadvertently received (for example, meeting with a consultant who is likely to possess inside information). Where firms choose to attend such meetings, they must consider additional practices to promote the identification of any inside information that could be received."[36]

As explained more fully later, most investment managers operate a "one-in-all-in" model – whereby as soon as anyone within the organisation becomes inside on a particular stock, that stock must then be promptly logged on the Restricted / Stop List; and, consequently, all trading[37] is precluded for so long as the stock remains on the List. One of the key reasons a firm would adopt this model is to ensure that no dealing takes place anywhere within the firm, whilst inside information is held in relation to the stock concerned – since, as outlined earlier

---

[36] TR 15/1 "Asset Management Firms and the Risk of Market Abuse", 2015.
[37] Both for funds / portfolios and personal account.

Insider dealing

in this chapter, the firm would otherwise be presumed to have insider dealt.

The efficacy of the "one-in-all-in" model relies heavily on the awareness of the investment professionals – to ensure that all inside situations are identified and duly logged on a timely basis.

Case study

By way of example, a portfolio manager (PM) attends a company meeting. During the meeting, the company's CFO over-steps the mark and divulges some (positive) inside information. PM simply does not appreciate that he has just received inside information. He returns to his office and places a large "buy" order in the equities of that company.

The trade instructed by PM is subsequently investigated by the regulator; and PM is alleged to have insider dealt. PM argues in his defence that he did not, in all good faith, realise that he was "inside" and that he is innocent.

While, in all innocence, PM may in fact not have identified the fact that he has received inside information at the meeting, that alone will not afford him (or, indeed, his firm) a defence to an allegation of insider dealing.

PM may also seek to argue that he was reasonably entitled to rely upon the fact that the CFO should not be selectively disclosing inside information[38]; and, therefore, that everything said by the CFO must, accordingly and by definition, have been non-inside information. In other words, PM might contend that he was reasonably entitled to assume that the CFO would not be committing market abuse (through the unlawful disclosure of inside information – discussed in the following chapter).

These further arguments would also likely fail.

Nor, incidentally, would PM have been able to rely, without more, upon any statement or confirmation made at the meeting by the CFO that no inside information had been disclosed. PM would, in any event,

---

[38] As to do so would likely constitute the "unlawful disclosure" offence, discussed in the next chapter.

always be expected to have applied his own mind to the issue; and formed an independent view. In short, an investment professional should never blindly or exclusively rely upon such an assurance from a company officer or sell-side adviser – without also applying their own judgement to the particular situation.

Cancellation or amendment of an existing order

A portfolio manager (PM1) places a large ("buy") trade for shares in ABC Plc. The trade is only partially executed when another portfolio manager in the same firm (PM2), unbeknown to PM1, receives inside information in relation to ABC Plc. What happens to the outstanding / open portion of the order?

Buy-side institutions will typically operate one of two (polar opposite) policies:

(1) allow the order to continue to be executed – on the basis that there would be a clear "audit trail" evidencing that the investment decision had been taken prior to PM2's / the firm's receipt of inside information; or

(2) require the outstanding portion of the order to be cancelled.

In our view, either of these approaches is acceptable. However, it is critical that, whichever policy is adopted, *no discretion is permitted*. In other words, the policy must be *fixed* and its application non-discretionary. No cherry-picking.

Option (1) can occasionally lead to a practical dilemma for firms – in circumstances where the executing broker reverts to the firm for further instructions on the execution of the outstanding portion of the order. It is very difficult for the firm to respond to any such requests – as it is inside at that point. In practice, it could therefore be challenging to disprove any allegation that any response was influenced by the inside information.

Option (2) would not present such a conundrum; and might be (marginally) viewed as reputationally preferable. [However, it is important to ensure that an option (2) policy legislates for (and prohibits) any cynical usage.]

For completeness, option (2) would not involve the "use" of the inside information. The cancellation is automatically triggered by the **mere fact of receipt of inside information** – with no relation whatsoever between the cancellation decision itself and the import of (i.e. the news within) the inside information (which might in any given case be positive, negative or neutral). In other words, it could not credibly be argued that there was here any "misuse" of, or unfair advantage of the benefit gained from, the inside information – as discussed in chapter 3 above.[39]

Non-issuer originated inside information

As outlined in the previous chapter, inside information need not have originated from the issuer itself. Accordingly (and by way of example), it is an offence to "front-run" – namely to take advantage of a significant impending (non-public and potentially market-moving) fund order by trading ahead on personal account (in the same stock), in anticipation of a share price movement.

Some useful rules of thumb

In practice, it can often be difficult to adjudge whether or not a particular proposed course of action falls on the right side of the "insider dealing" line.

One way of addressing such situations is by applying the following (admittedly non-technical, but nevertheless often instructive) "tests":

Counterparty test

- How would our counterparty likely react if, following the trade, they discovered that we knew what we knew at the time of transacting?
- How would we react if we were in the counterparty's shoes?

If there is any real prospect of your counterparty feeling unfairly aggrieved (as distinct from having simply suffered from a bad commercial bargain), then this should, at the very least, serve as a "red flag". A (free-and-easy) avenue for a disgruntled counterparty is to file

---

[39] See Recitals (23) and (24) of MAR.

a complaint with the regulator. Indeed, numerous enforcement cases have been precipitated by such "tip offs".[40]

Regulatory hindsight test

- If challenged, how comfortably could we explain this transaction to a regulator, applying hindsight?
- What (ideally, contemporaneous) evidence would we have to point to?

Again, any difficulty in answering these questions should be regarded as a "red flag"; and, at a minimum, warrant further expert consultation and consideration.

---

[40] For example, the FSA (as it then was) cases against *Morton and Parry* (2008).

7

UNLAWFUL DISCLOSURE

It is also an offence for a person to unlawfully disclose inside information.[41]

The offence

Unlawful disclosure of inside information arises where a person possesses inside information and discloses that information to any other person, *except where the disclosure is made in the normal exercise of an employment, profession or duties.*

As with insider dealing, this offence extends to those who know **or ought to know** that they possess inside information.

Notably, the unlawful disclosure offence does not require any form of "dealing". Indeed, the response (if any) by the recipient of the inside information is entirely irrelevant to the question of whether the unlawful disclosure offence has been committed. In other words, a person may have unlawfully disclosed inside information — notwithstanding that the recipient did not in fact act upon that information. Obviously, if the recipient *does* act on the inside information, (s)he will be exposed to a charge of insider dealing.

The underlying rationale for this offence is that it facilitates / leads to an un-level information playing field — an unfair advantage of which **could** thereafter be taken by the recipient.

---

[41] Articles 10 and 14 of MAR.

Unlawful disclosure

Dispelling a myth ...

As discussed in the previous chapter, most asset managers operate a "one-in-all-in" policy. In essence, this results in all employees being *deemed* to be inside on any stock which is logged on the Restricted / Stop List.

However, and contrary to a (mistaken) view held in certain quarters, this does **not** mean that individuals are at liberty to disclose inside information freely within the institution – not least, because this would be irreconcilable with the widely-adopted "need-to-know" policy (on which regulators remain very focused).

There is a huge difference between being *deemed* to be inside and being *actually* inside. From the regulator's perspective, and put simply, the greater the number of individuals who are *actually* privy to inside information, the greater the likelihood of a leak – inside information should therefore always be tightly controlled and contained.

In a thematic review focused on the risk of market abuse within asset managers, the FCA observed [our emphasis]:

"Most firms considered all employees to be restricted when inside information had been received by the firm and did not rely on the ability to restrict knowledge of inside information to particular individuals. ***All firms, however, had a policy to limit the sharing of inside information to those who needed to know****. In some firms, the 'need-to-know' policy was monitored by keeping a list of who knew what inside information.*

Limiting the number of people who have knowledge of inside information to those who need to know manages the risk of improper disclosure and reduces the risk of insider dealing*. Firms should consider how they can reduce these risks, which may include keeping documentation of who knows what inside information, particularly in sensitive cases."*[42]

As a practical matter, advice should always be sought on whether a proposed (internal or external) disclosure of inside information would be permissible as "made in the normal exercise of an employment,

---

[42] TR 15/1 "Asset Management Firms and the Risk of Market Abuse", 2015.

profession or duties". As a working principle, it should be assumed that this "carve-out" would be narrowly (restrictively) construed.

Simple practical illustrations

- A company's CFO discloses some inside information to an investor at a private meeting.
- A corporate financier friend divulges some inside information to you at a social event.
- A "wall-crossed" (i.e. inside) portfolio manager freely circulates inside information within his organisation.
- An investment bank providing an indication to a prospective placee as to the status of a book-building exercise.

Encouraging or inducing unlawful disclosure of inside information

While not a technical offence under MAR as such, it would be inadvisable for a person to positively encourage or induce an insider to selectively (unlawfully) disclose inside information. In the UK, such conduct could well be regarded as a breach of an applicable principle by the individual and/or their firm – for instance, a failure to: act with integrity or with due skill, care and diligence; or to observe proper standards of market conduct.

Case study

At a one-on-one company meeting, a portfolio manager (PM) asks the company's CEO to clarify whether a market rumour (that the company will shortly be coming to the market to raise funds) is in fact accurate.

As tempting as it may well have been to do so, this was not an appropriate question for PM to have asked in the circumstances. PM ought to have realised that a straight answer to his query (which should always, arguably, be prudently assumed) would inevitably result in the CEO's disclosure of inside information – namely, the confirmation or denial (as the case may be) of the market rumour. And that, in turn, would have left PM inside and therefore restricted. In other words, what did PM think he had to achieve by asking that question?!

Unlawful disclosure

As a general guiding principle, and for the reasons explained, any question[43] which, if answered directly, would likely result in the selective disclosure of inside information, is arguably an inappropriate question. Such conduct would risk being viewed as irresponsible; and (in the UK at least) potentially in contravention of a number of applicable principles.

---

[43] Whether posed at a company meeting or during any other private interaction with a listed issuer.

8
MARKET MANIPULATION

Backdrop

A number of market abuse offences are encapsulated within the broad heading of "market manipulation". The various market manipulation offences, summarised below, are of less obvious relevance to investment managers, given their specific role and responsibilities. On that basis, "market manipulation" is accorded only relatively cursory attention in this publication. Of course, that is not to be taken as signifying that market manipulation is an irrelevance or otherwise not important. Indeed, regulators have signalled that they will be pursuing more market manipulation cases in the future.

Case study

A fund manager's quarterly performance will improve if the valuation of his portfolio at the end of the quarter in question is higher rather than lower. He places a large order to buy relatively illiquid shares, which are also components of his portfolio, to be executed at or just before the close. His purpose is to position the price of the shares at a false, misleading, abnormal or artificial level. Such conduct is likely to be regarded as market manipulation.

Asset managers and investment professionals should therefore ensure that they are familiar with the market manipulation offences.

The offences

Key underpinning principles – a reminder

The various "market manipulation" offences are broadly underpinned by the Fundamental Principles that:

Market manipulation

- at any given time, the market (and its participants) has an accurate and not misleading impression of the price or supply of, or demand for, a particular financial instrument (or a related derivative);
- prices are not improperly secured at artificial levels; and
- demand is not improperly squeezed.

Market manipulation offences

Market manipulation comprises the following activities[44]:

(a) Entering into a transaction, placing an order to trade **or any other behaviour** which:

   i. gives, or is likely to give, **false or misleading signals** as to the supply of, demand for, or price of, a financial instrument; or

   ii. **secures, or is likely to secure, the price of one or several financial instruments at an abnormal or artificial level**.

   Unless the person entering into a transaction, placing an order or engaging in any other behaviour establishes that such activity was carried out **for legitimate reasons and conform with accepted market practice**[45].

(b) Entering into a transaction, placing an order to trade **or any other activity or behaviour** which **affects or is likely to affect the price of one or several financial instruments**; and which **employs a fictitious device or any other form or deception or contrivance**.

(c) **Disseminating information** through the media, including the Internet, or by any other means, which **gives, or is likely to give, false or misleading signals as to the supply of, demand for, or price of, a financial instrument**; or **secures, or is likely to secure, the price of one or several financial instruments at an abnormal or artificial level**, including the dissemination of rumours, **where**

---

[44] Article 12 of MAR.
[45] Annex I of MAR sets out a non-exhaustive list of indicators of manipulative behaviour relating to false or misleading signals and to price securing. Article 13 of MAR elaborates on the concept of an "accepted market practice"; and the criteria that a regulator may take into account in designating such a practice. A detailed account is beyond the scope of this publication.

the person who made the dissemination knew, or ought to have known, that the information was false or misleading.

(d) **Transmitting false or misleading information or providing false or misleading inputs** in relation to a benchmark, **where the person who made the transmission or provided the input knew or ought to have known that it was false or misleading**.

Legitimate reasons

The following factors are to be taken into account when considering whether behaviour is for "legitimate reasons" in relation to paragraph (a) above, and are indications that it is not:

(1) if the person has an actuating purpose behind the transaction to induce others to trade in, bid for or to position or move the price of, a financial instrument;

(2) if the person has another, illegitimate, reason behind the transactions, bid or order to trade; and

(3) if the transaction was executed in a particular way with the purpose of creating a false or misleading impression.

The following factors are to be taken into account when considering whether behaviour is for legitimate reasons in relation to article 12(1)(a) of the MAR, and are indications that it *is*:

(1) if the transaction is pursuant to a prior legal or regulatory obligation owed to a third party;

(2) if the transaction is executed in a way which takes into account the need for the market or auction platform as a whole to operate fairly and efficiently;

(3) the extent to which the transaction generally opens a new position, so creating an exposure to market risk, rather than closes out a position and so removes market risk; and

(4) if the transaction complied with the rules of the relevant trading venue about how transactions are to be executed in a proper way (for example, rules on reporting and executing cross-transactions).

Market manipulation

It is unlikely that the behaviour of trading venue users when dealing at times and in sizes most beneficial to them (whether for the purpose of long-term investment objectives, risk management or short-term speculation) and seeking the maximum profit from their dealings will **of itself** amount to manipulation. Such behaviour, generally speaking, improves the liquidity and efficiency of trading venues.[46]

It is unlikely that prices in the market which are trading outside their normal range will necessarily be indicative that someone has engaged in behaviour with the purpose of positioning prices at a distorted level. High or low prices relative to a trading range can be the result of the proper interplay of supply and demand.[47]

Some non-exhaustive examples

The following (non-exhaustive types of) behaviour shall be considered as market manipulation:

(i) The conduct by a person, or persons acting in collaboration, to secure a dominant position over the supply of or demand for a financial instrument which has, or is likely to have, the effect of fixing, directly or indirectly, purchase or sale prices or creates, or is likely to create, other unfair trading conditions.

(ii) The buying or selling of financial instruments, at the opening or closing of the market, which has, or is likely to have, the effect of misleading investors acting on the basis of the prices displayed, including the opening or closing prices.

(iii) The placing of orders to a trading venue, including any cancellation or modification thereof, by any available means of trading, including by electronic means, such as algorithmic and high-frequency trading strategies, and which has one of the effects referred to in paragraphs (a) or (b) above, by:

- disrupting or delaying the functioning of the trading system of the trading venue or being likely to do so;

---

[46] MAR 1.6.7G.
[47] MAR 1.6.8G.

- making it more difficult for other persons to identify genuine orders on the trading system of the trading venue or being likely to do so, including by entering orders which result in the overloading or destabilisation of the order book; or
- creating or being likely to create a false or misleading signal about the supply of, or demand for, or price of, a financial instrument, in particular by entering orders to initiate or exacerbate a trend.

(iv) The taking advantage of occasional or regular access to the traditional or electronic media by voicing an opinion about a financial instrument (or indirectly about its issuer) while having previously taken positions on that financial instrument and profiting subsequently from the impact of the opinions voiced on the price of that instrument, without having simultaneously disclosed that conflict of interest to the public in a proper and effective way.

The FCA's case against *Walter*[48] is illustrative. In summary, Walter wanted to sell a particular instrument. He was aware that algorithms were tracking the best bid and offer price. He therefore posted small bids in order to alter the price at which the algorithms were prepared to offer much larger sizes. He then traded to sell his position at these new prices (knowing that such an order would not interact with his own sell order). Although the algorithms had been programmed to act in this way, Walter's actions in altering the then best bid and offer price were judged to be manipulative, in particular because he had no intention or genuine economic interest in selling at the prices at which he was posting.

Practical application

As a practical matter, if there is any doubt as to whether a proposed course of action may be regarded as falling within any of the above offences, advice should be sought at the earliest opportunity.

If, following consultation with advisers, it is determined that the proposed course of action would not amount to a breach of any of these offences, it would be prudent to document the basis upon which that conclusion was reached.

---

[48] https://www.fca.org.uk/publication/final-notices/paul-axel-walter-2017.pdf

9

MARKET SOUNDINGS

Context

The number of inadvertent "wall-crossings" resulting from poorly controlled / disciplined sounding-out processes – *Einhorn / Greenlight* being a good case in point – had been troubling the regulators for some time (and not to mention the affected buy-side institutions which found themselves involuntarily "off-side" for an indeterminate period).

Such is their importance (and inherently high-risk profile), "market soundings" were therefore deemed to warrant specific legislative provision within MAR.

Market soundings – defined

A "market sounding" comprises the communication of information, prior to the announcement of a transaction, in order the gauge the interest of potential investors in a possible transaction; and the conditions relating to it, such as its potential size or pricing, to one or more potential investors by:

(a) an issuer;

(b) a secondary offeror of a financial instrument, in such quantity or value that the transaction is distinct from ordinary trading and involves a selling method based on the prior assessment of potential interest from potential investors; or

(c) a third party acting, with a mandate, on behalf, or on the account, of a person referred to in (a) or (b).

Disclosure of inside information made in the course of a market sounding shall be deemed to be made in the normal exercise of a person's employment, profession or duties – and therefore not

Market soundings

contravene the "unlawful disclosure" offence – where the DMP complies with the requirements set out below.[49]

Market sounding process

MAR[50] prescribes certain steps that must be taken by the DMP; and other measures by the market sounding recipient (MSR), in the context of a market sounding.

DMP requirements

A DMP shall, prior to conducting a market sounding, **specifically consider whether the market sounding will involve the disclosure of inside information**. The DMP shall make a written record of its conclusion and the reasons therefor; and provide such written records to the regulator upon request. This obligation shall apply to each disclosure of information throughout the course of the market sounding. The DMP shall update these written records accordingly.[51]

Before making any disclosure, the DMP shall[52]:

(a) obtain the consent of the MSR to receive inside information;

(b) inform the MSR that it is prohibited from using that information, or attempting to use that information, by acquiring or disposing of, for its own account or for the account of a third party, directly or indirectly, financial instruments relating to that information;

(c) inform the MSR that it is prohibited from using that information, or attempting to use that information, by cancelling or amending an order which has already been placed concerning a financial instrument to which the information relates; and

(d) inform the MSR that by agreeing to receive the information it is obliged to keep the information confidential.

The DMP shall make and maintain a record of all information given to the MSR and the identity of the potential investors to whom the

---

[49] Article 11.4 of MAR.
[50] Together with related RTS and Guidelines.
[51] Article 11.3 of MAR.
[52] Article 11.5 of MAR.

information has been disclosed, including but not limited to the legal and natural persons acting on behalf of the potential investor, and the date and time of each disclosure. The DMP shall provide that record to the regulator upon request.

Where information that has been disclosed in the course of a market sounding ceases to be inside information according to the assessment of the DMP, the DMP shall inform the MSR accordingly, as soon as possible.

Wherever possible, the DMP shall ensure that recorded lines are used for a market sounding (and any follow-up conversations).[53]

Additionally, DMPs must, amongst other things, disclose the following to the MSR ahead of any market sounding (considered by the DMP to involve the disclosure of inside information):

(a) a statement clarifying that the communication takes place for the purposes of a market sounding;

(b) where the market sounding is conducted by recorded telephone lines, or audio or video recording is being used, a statement indicating that the conversation is recorded and the consent of the person receiving the market sounding to be recorded;

(c) a request for and a confirmation from the contacted person that the DMP is communicating with the person entrusted by the potential investor to receive the market sounding and the reply to that request;

(d) a statement clarifying that, if the contacted person agrees to receive the market sounding, that person will receive information that the DMP considers to be inside information;

(e) where possible, an estimation of when the information will cease to be inside information, the factors that may alter that estimation and, in any case, information about the manner in which the MSR will be informed of any change in such an estimation;

(f) a request for the consent of the MSR to receive inside information, and the reply to that request; and

---

[53] RTS 2016/960.

(g) where the consent required under point (f) is given, the information being disclosed for the purposes of the market sounding, identifying the information considered by the DMP to be inside information.

DMPs have similar obligations in respect of market soundings *not* deemed to involve the disclosure of inside information.

DMPs must also maintain a list of all natural and legal persons to whom information[54] has been disclosed; together with the date and time of each communication of information which has taken place in the course of or following the market sounding.

MSR requirements

While much of the procedural burden of market soundings falls upon DMPs, MSRs have their own obligations.

A MSR must assess (*and document*) whether it is in possession of inside information or when it ceases to be in possession of inside information – **notwithstanding** (and independent of) the requirement for DMPs to communicate at the outset their "inside or not" assessment to the MSRs.

Such independent assessment shall take into consideration as relevant factors: the DMP's assessment and all the information available to the individual(s), function or body entrusted within the MSR to conduct that assessment, including information obtained from sources other than the DMP. In conducting that assessment, the individual(s), function or body should not be required to access information behind any information barrier established within the MSR.

Where the MSR has assessed that it is in possession of inside information as a result of a market sounding, the MSR should identify all the issuers and financial instruments to which it believes that inside information relates.

Similarly, further to the DMP's notification that the information disclosed in the course of the market sounding is no longer inside information, the MSR should independently assess (and document)

---

[54] Note: *any* information; and not only inside information.

whether it is still in possession of inside information taking into consideration the DMP's assessment and all the information available to the individual(s), function or body entrusted within the MSR to conduct that assessment, including information obtained from other sources than the DMP. In conducting that assessment, the individual(s), function or body should not be required to access information behind any information barrier established within the MSR.

Additionally, MSRs should establish, implement and maintain internal procedures that are appropriate and proportionate to the scale, size and nature of their business activity, to: (a) ensure that, where the MSR designates a specific person or a contact point to receive market soundings, that information is made available to the DMP; (b) ensure that the information received in the course of the market sounding is internally communicated only through pre-determined reporting channels and on a need-to-know basis; (c) ensure that the individual(s), function or body entrusted to assess whether the MSR is in possession of inside information as a result of the market sounding are clearly identified and properly trained to that purpose; (d) manage and control the flow of inside information arising from the market sounding within the MSR and its staff, in order for the MSR and its staff to comply with articles 8 (insider dealing) and 10 (unlawful disclosure) of MAR.

MSRs should ensure that the staff receiving and processing the information obtained in the course of the market sounding are properly trained on the relevant internal procedures and on the prohibitions arising from being in possession of inside information. The training should be appropriate and proportionate to the scale, size and nature of the MSR's business activity.

FAQs

The market soundings regime has given rise to a number of questions of interpretation – for example:

Is the communication of any information caught, or must it be inside information?

The market soundings regime is not restricted to the sharing of **inside** information.

Market soundings

What is "prior to the announcement"?

A statement to the market that a transaction is in contemplation does not amount to the announcement of the transaction itself. Rather, that would require an announcement as to the price, size, key details, and timing of a transaction. In other words, it is the moment at which the company stops deciding what to do, and announces to the world its express intentions. In the UK, many equity market participants have taken the view that this could be the moment at which the Intention to Float announcement is made in an initial public offering (IPO) scenario.

What amounts to "gauging the interest of potential investors"?

Dialogue with investors in order to understand their intentions relating to a potential transaction is caught. Sometimes this can be easy to identify – for instance, if a "testing the waters" exercise is being undertaken. In other circumstances, it can be more difficult. What if the company intends to present at an industry conference, knowing that a transaction is contemplated, but without mentioning that transaction? Such circumstances will be somewhat fact-specific, but in practice, caution should be exercised if it is objectively evident that a conversation is aimed at understanding the future intention of investors. Any such conversations should only be undertaken on a "market soundings" basis.

Practicalities

Investment managers have adopted a range of protocols for market soundings. Some institutions require, as a firm policy, that any and all market sounding enquiries received by investment professionals should immediately be deflected to compliance (or another independent function).

Others continue to allow (either all or designated senior) portfolio managers to receive market soundings. Certain firms have resolved not to receive any market soundings whatsoever – on the basis of their own cost-benefit-analyses.

There is no single "right" approach. Clearly, whichever model is adopted, it is essential that all relevant personnel are familiar with their firm's own policy and processes.

Market soundings

Vigilance should also be exercised in relation to initial calls (exploring the possibility of a wall-crossing / market sounding) – given the risk of inside information being inadvertently imparted during such enquiries[55].

Occasionally, it may not have been made clear (by, say, a sell-side bank acting for an issuer) whether or not a proposed dialogue will constitute a market sounding. In such circumstances, the buy-side firm can quite properly seek clarification from the enquirer as to whether this will be a market sounding.

A note of caution …

Clearly, an enquiry by or on behalf of a listed issuer may fall outside of the technical "market sounding" definition – for instance, if no transaction announcement will be made.

While the prescriptive requirements outlined above will not therefore apply, it is nevertheless vital that those on the receiving end of such enquiries nevertheless remain vigilant and well-attuned to the risk of receiving inside information.

As always, where there is any doubt, advice should be sought at the earliest opportunity.

---

[55] As was, arguably, the case in *Einhorn / Greenlight* – see further chapter 12.

10
LOANS AND OTHER "OUT-OF-SCOPE" INSTRUMENTS

Loans and other "out-of-scope" instruments (collectively, **"LOOI"**) are not regulated under MAR. However, this does not necessarily mean that "anything goes" in the LOOI markets.

Industry body guidelines

Loan Market Association (LMA)

The LMA has issued guidelines in relation to the trading of loans in the secondary market (the "LMA Guidelines")[56]. The LMA Guidelines explain that:

"Participants [in the secondary loan market] are expected to behave with integrity towards the loan market ... most participants in the loan market will be [UK-] regulated entities, and therefore subject to regulatory principles and standards both in their handling of information as well as their activities in the loan market.

All market participants may trade loans on the basis of information that is available to the whole syndicate – Syndicate Confidential Information (SCI). This includes trading loans with counterparties who were entitled to receive such SCI but chose not to.

Generally though, market participants should not trade on material information which has not been made available to the whole of a lending syndicate – Borrower Confidential Information (BCI). Information will typically be considered 'material' where, if it were known to the entire

---

[56] Transparency Guidelines (2012). It is understood that the Guidelines are in the process of being reviewed.

Loans and other "out-of-scope" instruments

syndicate, it would significantly impact the price of the relevant loan. This could, for example, include ... information received as a result of membership of a steering committee."

According to the LMA, best practice includes:

(a) market participants may trade loans based on SCI; and

(b) steering committee members should not generally trade loans based on BCI (even where the trade counterparty has access to the same level of BCI).

Notwithstanding point (b), and *"in order to facilitate restructurings and encourage the involvement of key major lenders, there may be circumstances where a member of a steering committee or a supporting lender possessing BCI may reasonably make a judgement (subject to applicable law) that it is consistent with appropriate standards of professional integrity and fair dealings to trade, regardless of whether its counterparty is also in possession of or has the ability to receive such BCI, provided that:*

(i) the relevant lender discloses to the counterparty that it is in possession of BCI (thought the BCI itself need not be disclosed);

(ii) in the event that the counterparty enters into any downstream trade of the loans so traded, it will disclose to the downstream counterparty the fact that some or all of the relevant loans were purchased from a lender holding BCI unless the relevant counterparty acting reasonably (and consistently with appropriate standards of professional integrity and fair dealings) concludes that in all the circumstances (including the period which has elapsed since the original trade) there is no longer any need to do so; and

(iii) the relevant lender has reasonably made a judgement (consistently with appropriate standards of professional integrity and fair dealings) that the transaction will not adversely affect other members of the syndicate / market."

In practice, the mechanism commonly adopted in relation to points (i) to (iii) above will be the execution, by both parties, of a "big-boy" letter. In essence, "big-boy" letters are intended to ensure that the purchaser enters the transaction "eyes wide open" – confirming its knowledge and acceptance of the fact that the seller possesses a material informational advantage, but clearly indicating its willingness to transact nonetheless.[57]

Other perspectives

At least one other industry body, the Alternative Investment Management Association (AIMA), has argued that the LMA Guidelines are *"unduly restrictive"*[58] [our emphasis]:

"The Guidelines accept that loans may be traded by parties holding SCI, and accept that this is the case even where one party has chosen not to receive or does not, in practice, hold such information. The standard LMA terms and conditions contain Big Boy language (Non-Reliance and Independent Investigation) which is designed to protect a party from liability to the other party in circumstances where there is an information disparity. Although there is an asymmetry of information and although that asymmetry could (in theory, at least) impact the price at which the debt trades, this approach appears acceptable to the LMA. **It is uncertain why a similar approach would not be acceptable in relation to BCI, provided that the parties to the trade enter into the trade with their eyes open** *and subject to enhanced Big Boy language. The market has ... worked with and accepted the risk of 'Big Boy' confirmations from the outset ..."*

In support of this view, AIMA goes on to point out that:

- the loan market is a professional market, with counterparties who will almost all have carried out sophisticated credit analysis on any credit in which they invest;
- LMA's existing terms of trade allow disparity of information between counterparties where one is public and the other private with respect to SCI; and
- institutions should continue to have the freedom to contract on such terms where the disparity is caused by one institution having BCI.

---

[57] Note: "Big-boy" letters are not typically used in the context of listed securities.
[58] AIMA Note on Sound Practice in the Secondary Loan Market, March 2013.

It is difficult to take issue with the inherent logic of these arguments; and it is to be hoped that they are addressed and reflected accordingly in any revised LMA Guidelines.

Don't forget the Principles (which still apply even if MAR doesn't) ...

To recap, the LMA Guidelines acknowledge that: *"Participants [in the secondary loan market] are expected to behave with integrity towards the loan market ... most participants in the loan market will be [UK-] regulated entities, and therefore subject to regulatory principles and standards both in their handling of information as well as their activities in the loan market."*

The most obviously relevant regulatory principles in this context are: acting with integrity; acting with due skill, care and diligence; and observing proper standards of market conduct. The regulator can, and does, bring enforcement cases purely for breach of principles – including in circumstances involving inappropriate market conduct which, for whatever reason, happens to fall outside the ambit of MAR – such as *Kyprios*, discussed in chapter 2.

As discussed earlier, the Fundamental Principles (discussed in chapter 3) can serve as a useful proxy for the interpretation of "proper standards of market conduct". As a general rule of thumb, where a proposed course of conduct could be perceived as offending against the Fundamental Principles, it might prudently be assumed that such a scenario will attract regulatory interest and scrutiny – **irrespective of whether or not it technically falls within the scope of MAR**.

11
COMPANY MEETINGS / DIALOGUE

Introduction

Company meetings / dialogue represent an important element of many firms' investment processes. While such meetings / dialogue might be considered very beneficial on the one hand, they involve inherent risk on the other. This risk – of selectively receiving inside information – is not a new phenomenon. However, in the wake of various high-profile cases, such as *Greenlight / Einhorn*, it has of late attracted increased focus and attention.

A small number of firms have concluded that the perceived benefits are outweighed by the risks; and accordingly preclude their investment professionals from attending such meetings / dialogue.

For the majority of institutions that continue to partake in such meetings / dialogue, **it is essential that awareness levels and vigilance remain high**. As already highlighted, it is vital that investment professionals are able to identify inside information – ignorance or absent-mindedness will not afford a defence to a charge of insider dealing under MAR.

"If firms receive inside information but it is not identified as such, there is a significant risk that this information is acted on in breach of market abuse rules. Firms should consider the benefit relative to the risk of attending meetings where there is a significant possibility that inside information might be inadvertently received (for example, meeting with a consultant who is likely to possess inside information). Where firms choose to attend such meetings, they must consider additional practices to promote the identification of any inside information that could be received."[59]

Further, asset managers cannot reasonably assume that anything and everything that they are told by an issuer will not be inside information.

---

[59] TR 15/1 "Asset Management Firms and the Risk of Market Abuse".

Company meetings / dialogue

Rather, investment professionals are expected to apply their own minds in such situations. A practical case in point is covered in the following chapter (*Einhorn / Greenlight*).

A case study from chapter 7 is repeated here, given its particular relevance in this context too.

Case study

At a one-on-one company meeting, a portfolio manager (PM) asks the company's CEO to clarify whether a market rumour (that the company will shortly be coming to the market to raise funds) is in fact accurate.

As tempting as it may well have been to do so, this was not an appropriate question for PM to have asked in the circumstances. PM ought to have realised that a straight answer to his query (which should always, arguably, be prudently assumed) would inevitably result in the CEO's disclosure of inside information – namely, the confirmation or denial (as the case may be) of the market rumour. And that, in turn, would have left PM inside and therefore restricted. In other words, what did PM think he had to achieve by asking that question?!

As a general guiding principle, and for the reasons explained, any question[60] which, if answered directly, would likely result in the selective disclosure of inside information, is arguably an inappropriate question. Such conduct would risk being viewed as irresponsible; and (in the UK at least) potentially in contravention of a number of applicable principles.

An occasional challenge from portfolio managers to this suggested general principle is: "What's the point of ever actually attending company meetings, if I can't ask questions like this?!"

This question, in turn, prompts the further (and admittedly philosophical) question: "What is the point of company meetings?" – a question that could quite conceivably be posed to investment professionals during a regulatory supervision or thematic visit.

---

[60] For instance, whether posed at a company meeting or during any other private dialogue with a listed issuer.

What is the point of a company meeting?

Clearly, the answer to this question is **not** "to elicit inside information"! Investment professionals will typically respond with one or more of the following:

- To assess the credibility of Management.
- To obtain some further colour / explanation on a discrete issue (where which colour / explanation would **not** constitute inside information).
  - For instance, it may be to obtain the final small piece of a complex investment "mosaic" – which would be of no consequence to a "reasonable investor".
- To communicate the investor's views / expectations to Management.

It is self-evidently crucial that investment professionals participating in company meetings / dialogue are very clear as to what information it is legitimate for them to seek to derive; and conversely, as to the "red lines" which must not be crossed.

Managing the inherent risks

Some asset managers require (or at least suggest) that investment professionals who attend company meetings clarify at the outset that they do not wish to receive any inside information. This can serve to help focus the minds of company officials (notwithstanding that their minds should be focused in any event!). However, while undoubtedly helpful, such statements **cannot** simply be relied upon to assume that all information subsequently imparted at the meeting will not amount to inside information. As always, investment professionals must still maintain a high state of vigilance to the risk of inadvertent disclosure by the issuer (or its representatives).

Certain firms will prohibit participation on company meetings / dialogue during close periods – as the risk of disclosure of inside information is perceived to be greater in the lead-up to a results announcement by the issuer. Other firms will take a more permissive approach – albeit, typically subject to an edict for even higher levels of vigilance from the individuals concerned.

12
EINHORN / GREENLIGHT

Introduction

Numerous references have already been made to the *David Einhorn / Greenlight* case. While published in 2012, it remains a seminal (and instructive) case – for buy-side professionals, in particular.

This chapter summarises the salient facts of the case; and then draws out the salutary "take-aways" for investment professionals.

While this case pre-dates the implementation of MAR, it remains instructive nonetheless – since the key issues and underlying principles are equally applicable in a MAR context.

Executive factual summary

David Einhorn was the owner, President and sole portfolio manager of Greenlight Capital Inc (Greenlight). Greenlight was an investment management firm based in the United States. Greenlight managed investments held by various entities (the Greenlight Funds). Several of the Greenlight Funds had shareholdings in Punch Taverns Plc (Punch). The Greenlight Funds first acquired shares in Punch on 16 June 2008 and, by June 2009, the Funds owned 13.3% of Punch's issued share capital.

On Monday 15 June 2009, Punch announced a transaction to issue new equity in order to raise approximately £375 million of capital (the "**Transaction**"). Merrill Lynch International (MLI) was joint book runner and co-sponsor on the Transaction. Prior to the announcement of the Transaction, various shareholders and potential investors had been wall-crossed by MLI. Specific wall-crossing procedures were in place for Punch's existing large US-based shareholders whereby they would be asked to agree the terms of a non-disclosure agreement (NDA).

On Monday 8 June 2009 (seven days before the announcement of the Transaction), MLI raised with Greenlight the subject of a possible equity issuance by Punch and invited Greenlight to be wall-crossed in relation to Punch. Mr Einhorn refused this request, but a call was arranged for the following day between Punch's management and Mr Einhorn on a non-wall-crossed basis.

On Tuesday 9 June 2009, the MLI broker and Punch management proceeded to have a telephone conference call with Mr Einhorn (the **"Punch Call"**).

Even though the Punch Call was expressly set up on a "non-wall-crossed" basis, inside information was disclosed to Mr Einhorn during the call. The inside information disclosed to Mr Einhorn was that Punch was at an advanced stage of the process towards the issuance of a significant amount of new equity, probably within a timescale of around a week, with the principal purpose of repaying Punch's convertible bond and creating headroom with respect to certain covenants in Punch's securitisation vehicles.

Immediately following the Punch Call, Mr Einhorn directed that Greenlight traders sell the Greenlight Funds' entire shareholding in Punch. The decision to sell was solely Mr Einhorn's. Mr Einhorn decided to sell on the basis of the inside information he received on the Punch Call (albeit not solely on this basis). Between 9 June and 12 June 2009, Greenlight sold 11.65 million shares in Punch and thereby reduced the Greenlight Funds' stake from 13.3% to 8.98%.

The Transaction was announced to the market on 15 June 2009. Following the announcement of the Transaction, the price of Punch's shares fell by 29.9%. Greenlight's sale of Punch shares prior to the announcement of the Transaction had resulted in loss avoidance of approximately £5.8 million for the Greenlight Funds.

The FSA (Financial Services Authority) – the FCA's predecessor – considered this to be a serious case of market abuse by Mr Einhorn, in particular for the following reasons:

(i) Mr Einhorn occupied a prominent position as President of Greenlight – a high-profile hedge fund.

(ii) Mr Einhorn was an experienced trader and portfolio manager. He had over 15 years of experience running an investment management firm and should therefore be held to the highest standards of conduct and the highest levels of accountability.

(iii) Given Mr Einhorn's position and experience, it **should have been apparent to him** that the information he received on the Punch Call was confidential and price-sensitive information that gave rise to legal and regulatory risk. The Punch Call was unusual in that it was a discussion with management following a refusal to be wall-crossed. In the circumstances **Mr Einhorn should have been especially vigilant in assessing the information he received**. It was a serious error of judgement on Mr Einhorn's part to make the decision after the Punch Call to sell Greenlight's shares in Punch **without first seeking any compliance or legal advice** despite the ready availability of such resources within Greenlight.

(iv) Greenlight's trading took place over a period of four days and represented a large part of the daily volume traded in Punch shares over that period. Such significant trading in a stock on the basis of inside information severely undermines confidence in the market. The trading was highly visible to market participants.

(v) The trading resulted in loss avoidance for the Greenlight Funds of £5.8 million. Mr Einhorn had significant personal investment in the Greenlight Funds.

Despite being a serious case of market abuse which merited the imposition of a substantial financial penalty, **the market abuse was not deliberate or reckless**. **Mr Einhorn did not believe that the information that he had received was inside information, and he did not intend to commit market abuse.** Nevertheless, the FSA considered Mr Einhorn's error of judgement to be a serious failure to act in accordance with the standards reasonably expected of market participants.

As a result, Einhorn was convicted of insider dealing and fined £3,638,000 – £638,000 of which represented the disgorgement of financial benefit arising from the market abuse.

Information disclosed to Einhorn / Greenlight

Prior to the Punch Call

On Monday 8 June 2009, Andrew Osborne (the MLI MD who led the corporate broking account for Punch) had a telephone conversation with an analyst at Greenlight. He said that the call was a post-road show follow-up call, and he raised the subject of a possible equity issuance by Punch and asked the analyst if Greenlight would agree to be wall-crossed. The wall-crossing request was referred to Mr Einhorn. Mr Einhorn would not agree to Greenlight being wall-crossed and this decision was relayed back to Mr Osborne via the analyst. Mr Osborne attempted to persuade Greenlight to be wall-crossed, but this was not agreed and instead a call was set up for the following day between Greenlight and Punch management on an "open" basis.

On one view, the inside information line had already been crossed at this point – a point raised by many market observers.

During the Punch Call

On Tuesday 9 June, Mr Osborne and Punch management participated in the Punch Call with Mr Einhorn and the Greenlight analyst. The Punch Call lasted for approximately 45 minutes and involved a considerable amount of discussion between Punch management and Greenlight.

The inside information received by Mr Einhorn on the Punch Call was that Punch was at an advanced stage of the process towards the issuance of a significant amount of new equity, probably within a timescale of around a week, with the principal purpose of repaying Punch's convertible bond and creating headroom with respect to certain covenants in Punch's securitisation vehicles. The Punch Call had to be considered in the context in which it took place and in its entirety:

(i) With regard to context, Mr Einhorn knew in advance of the Punch Call that MLI wanted to wall-cross Greenlight in relation to Punch. When Mr Osborne spoke to the Greenlight analyst and asked Greenlight to agree to be wall-crossed, he had said that the wall-crossing related to Punch. Mr Osborne and the Greenlight analyst had also discussed Punch issuing equity on the same telephone call.

(ii) The Punch Call had to be considered as a whole. The particular pieces of information that are said to amount to inside information must be read as part of the entire conversation. The merits of Punch issuing equity form the subject matter of the majority of the call. Punch management and Mr Osborne attempted to persuade Mr Einhorn of the merits of an equity issuance and discussed the risks to the company of not issuing equity. There was no discussion of any other possible new approach to address risks that Punch may take.

Particular points of information that were disclosed to Mr Einhorn during the Punch Call included:

First: Mr Einhorn was told that the amount of any possible equity issuance would need to be about £350 million in order to repay the convertible and create 10% headroom in the securitisations. This information was offered by Mr Osborne:

> "Einhorn: So, would you – as you pencil that out, what do those amounts turn out to be?
>
> Osborne: Something like 350 sterling.
>
> Einhorn: 350 million sterling?
>
> Osborne: If you were – if you were roughly to sort of work on the basis that you kinda took out the – the converts and that is something that gives you, say, 10% headroom in within both of the covenants, filed covenants."

This disclosed that the principal purpose of the issuance would be to repay the convertible bond and create headroom in the securitisations, and that the sum of the issuance under consideration was of a very significant size; Punch was not considering a small equity issuance in the sum of, for instance, around £50 million. Whilst Mr Osborne did not give the sum of £350 million as a definitive figure, what he said to Mr Einhorn made it clear that the transaction was to raise a sum of equity that would be of considerable size relative to Punch's market capitalisation (Punch's market capitalisation at the time of the Punch Call was approximately £400 million).

Second: Mr Einhorn was told that an NDA would last for less than a week. Mr Osborne offered to give Mr Einhorn a *"time frame"* in respect of an NDA and when questioned by Mr Einhorn on what that would be, Mr Osborne stated *"Well, within less than a, kind of, week."*

Whilst an NDA does not confirm that a transaction is definitely going to take place within a certain timescale, it does disclose anticipated timing and, in these circumstances, it informed Mr Einhorn that the issuance was at an advanced stage.

Third: Mr Einhorn was told that Punch was consulting with all of its major shareholders, and that there was broad support for an equity issuance, thus also indicating that the issuance was at an advanced stage and likely to proceed. Mr Osborne said:

> *"Really it's fair to say like, consulting with all of the – the major shareholders in terms of taking, you know, taking into account their views...*
>
> *... a number of people have sort of signed NDAs because we had a bit more open conversations ...*
>
> *... I think it's fair to say that, you know, broadly, mostly all the shareholders are supportive."*

The reference to other NDAs further indicated that the issuance was likely to take place within a short period of time.

In isolation, none of the above points would (in the context of the Punch Call) amount to inside information. *However, taken together, these points did constitute inside information particularly because they disclosed to Mr Einhorn the purpose and anticipated size and timing of the issuance.*

Despite assertions made during the call by Punch management that they were considering their options and that no formal decisions had been made, *this did not detract from the essential information* disclosed during the call, namely that they were at an advanced stage of the process towards the issuance of a significant amount of new equity, probably within the timescale of around a week, with the principal purpose of repaying Punch's convertible bond and creating headroom with respect to certain covenants in Punch's securitisation vehicles.

In other words, it was necessary to look through the mere assertions to the reality (and context) of the situation. The actual import of the dialogue "trumped" the disclaimer-like statements from Punch management – substance prevailed over form.

Summary of Einhorn's representations in defence

It is instructive to consider various of Mr Einhorn's defence representations and the manner in which they were addressed by the FSA.

Information disclosed on the Punch Call

Mr Einhorn made representations that:

(i) On a fair view of the Punch Call, taken as a whole and in context, and bearing in mind relevant market practice, no inside information was conveyed. Although the pros and cons of Punch potentially issuing equity were discussed on the Punch Call, the discussion was high-level and conceptual. Punch's management invited Mr Einhorn's views and engaged in debate with him, and the discussion ended inconclusively. Punch's management made it clear that they were considering different alternatives, that no decisions had been made regarding an equity issuance or other course of action, and that Punch was continuing to operate on a "business as usual" basis.

(ii) Even on the FSA's case there was no single statement of inside information; rather, the information comprised various comments scattered throughout the 45-minute call. Since Mr Einhorn was not aware of what Punch was actually planning or doing, he therefore had to interpret the overall information provided to him, taking the Punch Call as a whole. Mr Einhorn was entitled to expect, having refused to sign an NDA and be wall-crossed, that he would not be given inside information. Although this did not mean that he could act on inside information if he received it, in order to know whether he had received it he interpreted what he was told in light of that expectation.

Further, there were a number of experienced professionals on the call, who were aware of Punch's plans, none of whom raised any concern that inside information had been disclosed, even when Mr Einhorn stated that Greenlight might sell its Punch shares. This suggested that nothing said on the call should be interpreted as constituting inside information.

(iii) It would not be fair to require Mr Einhorn, or any reasonable investor, to deduce that he had been given inside information by making inferences and assumptions, and ignoring the plain meanings of the words spoken to him. Mr Einhorn was told that an NDA would last for less than a week, not that an equity issuance was less than a week away. He was not told what the NDA covered. He did not understand this to mean that an equity issuance was taking place imminently, particularly since an NDA does not indicate that a transaction is about to occur, and that a timescale of a week, as opposed to a day, would indicate that any transaction was not yet at an advanced stage. The fact that Punch management wanted him to sign an NDA suggested matters were still at the discussion phase. The conversation was presented as a hypothetical back and forth, and included a number of "disclaimers" from Punch management that it was purely conceptual. Mr Einhorn took Punch management at their word.

(iv) None of the parties on the call thought that inside information had been disclosed. This supports the view that, as a matter of objective fact, no inside information was disclosed as the information disclosed would not indicate to a reasonable investor that an event may reasonably have been expected to occur.

(v) Even if inside information was, as a matter of objective fact, disclosed to Mr Einhorn, he did not understand it. He did not know what Punch was going to do after the call because the inside information, as formulated by the FSA, was not a conclusion that he drew. In his view he had simply participated in a conversation about the potential issuance of equity at some future time, about which Punch management had made no decisions.

The FSA found that:

(i) Taking the Punch Call as a whole and in context, it was sufficiently clear that an equity issuance was reasonably to be expected to occur imminently. Punch management's comments to the contrary made that no less apparent when taken in context.

(ii) While there was no single statement of inside information, and some interpretation was required, the clear interpretation of the comments made on the Punch Call disclosed inside information.

(iii) *Reasonable investors are expected to interpret comments made to them in an appropriate manner, which may sometimes mean understanding more than the precise words spoken, or interpreting certain comments in light of the context. If it is sufficiently clear that a discussion is not, in fact, merely conceptual, even express words to the contrary will not prevent inside information from being given.* In the specific circumstances of the Punch Call, it was clear that the equity issuance was imminent and that the reference to a timetable for the NDA disclosed the anticipated timetable for the issuance.

(iv) The fact that none of the parties to the call raised concerns regarding the disclosure of inside information does not affect the objective test of whether the information disclosed was inside information. In the FSA's view it was.

(v) Mr Einhorn interpreted and understood the inside information disclosed, notwithstanding that he did not believe that it was inside information.

Inside information

Mr Einhorn made representations that:

(i) the information alleged by the FSA to have been disclosed on the Punch Call did not in any event amount to inside information;

(ii) the equity issuance was not reasonably expected to occur at the time of the Punch Call; and

(iii) the information lacked sufficient detail to be "specific". It lacked detail, such as regarding the type of shares to be issued, and how and with whom they were to be placed. It was therefore not possible to draw a conclusion as to whether the effect on the share price would be to increase or decrease it.

The FSA has found that:

(i) The information disclosed to Mr Einhorn on the Punch Call did amount to inside information, for the reasons set out above.

(ii) Although the equity issuance was not certain to occur, at the time of the Punch Call, taking into account, among other factors, the advanced stage of preparation of the transaction, it was reasonably expected to occur.

(iii) Taking into account Punch's circumstances and the information about it which was already generally available, the information disclosed, which included the anticipated size, purpose and timing of an equity issuance, contained sufficient detail to enable a conclusion to be drawn as to the possible effect on the share price. The information was therefore "specific".

Dealing "on the basis of" inside information[61]

Mr Einhorn made representations that:

(i) Even if inside information was disclosed on the call, he did not deal on the basis of it. Although there was a presumption that he did so, the evidence here showed both that he did not interpret the call in a way that gave him that information and that in fact he traded for other reasons. Mr Einhorn did not understand the inside information disclosed, and therefore did not trade on the basis of a conclusion that he did not reach. His reasons for trading did not include, as a material factor, an appreciation of an imminent equity issuance. He did not dispute that he traded on the basis of the Punch Call, but stated that this was because the call made him lose faith in Punch as an investment, with which he was already unhappy. In particular, Punch's CEO stated that the stock was fairly valued at its then-current price, which Mr Einhorn found very surprising, and that there were "pluses and

---

[61] MAR replaced this formulation with "(mis-)used inside information to deal". However, the findings remain instructive.

minuses" unknown to the market that might mean the stock price would be discounted if the market knew. Overall, he found Punch management's tone to be surprisingly negative, and he began to doubt Greenlight's understanding of Punch. Given Punch's troubled nature and the relatively small size of the position compared to Greenlight's overall portfolio (less than 2%), he did not believe it made sense to stay invested when there were better uses for Greenlight's capital.

(ii) The manner of Greenlight's actual trading evidences that it did not trade "on the basis" of the alleged inside information. The trading was not aggressive, and in the end Greenlight still suffered a big loss at the time of the announcement and subsequent price drop, since Greenlight still owned two-thirds of its previous total amount of shares. If Mr Einhorn had understood that Punch was planning an imminent equity issuance, he either would have sold much more aggressively or held all of his shares in order to vote against the issuance and prevent it from going ahead.

The FSA has found that:

(i) As set out above, Mr Einhorn did understand the inside information disclosed to him. In the view of the FSA he has not rebutted the presumption that he dealt on the basis of that information. Although the FSA accepts that Mr Einhorn may have had more than one reason for trading, he has not shown that the equity issuance did not play a material part in that decision.

(ii) While Greenlight's selling was not as aggressive as it could have been, it still disposed of around one-third of its Punch shares within a matter of days, resulting in an avoidance of loss of over £5 million.

Section 123 of the Act[62]

Mr Einhorn made representations that:

(i) He took all reasonable precautions and exercised all due diligence to avoid committing, and reasonably believed that he had not committed, market abuse. He refused to be wall-crossed and relied on Punch management and the other insiders on the Punch Call not to give him inside information, or to tell him if they inadvertently had done so. None of the experienced parties on the call raised any concerns, even after he stated that he was considering selling Punch shares. Punch management told him that they were talking only in general terms and having an in-concept discussion – as a matter of market practice it was reasonable for him to place considerable weight on those disclaimers. Further, towards the end of the call he asked if the decision to issue equity had been made and was told that no formal decision had been made, and that the firm was consulting with various parties. He was also still being told at the end of the call that he was not wall-crossed. He took these comments as confirmation that he was "nowhere close" to having inside information.

(ii) He did not consult with internal or external compliance staff because he believed, reasonably and in good faith, that there was nothing to consult about. Further, the sell order was relayed to the trader who served as Greenlight UK's compliance officer, and the sales were vetted by Greenlight's in-house counsel to make sure that the necessary regulatory filings were made.

The FSA has found that:

(i) Although Mr Einhorn's approach to the Punch Call is not criticised, following the call Mr Einhorn should have been aware that he had been given inside information, or at the very least that there was a risk of this. He had a responsibility to consider whether the information received during the call constituted inside information before instructing the sale of shares. Given that the call took place following Mr Einhorn's refusal to sign an NDA, Mr Einhorn should

---

[62] A defence under the pre-MAR regime – which no longer exists under MAR. However, again, the findings are nevertheless instructive.

have been even more diligent than usual in considering whether inside information had been disclosed to him before selling. Having received the information, although it is accepted that he did not believe that it was inside information, before dealing he should have taken steps to ensure that it was not, such as obtaining compliance or legal advice, or contacting Punch management again to specifically clarify whether the information he had been given was inside information. Although he was entitled to give some weight to the fact that neither Punch nor its corporate advisers raised any concerns either during or immediately after the call, that does not remove *the obligation on Mr Einhorn to remain alert to the risk, make his own assessment of any information he received*, and take steps as necessary to confirm it. That the trading was subject to Greenlight's usual processes for dealing does not mitigate these failings.

(ii) In the absence of these necessary further steps, it cannot be said that Mr Einhorn took all reasonable precautions and exercised all due diligence to avoid committing market abuse, nor that his honestly-held belief that he was not committing market abuse was reasonable.

Penalty

Mr Einhorn made representations that:

(i) Deterrence should not be a significant factor in determining the penalty in this case since there is no evidence of a material risk of these circumstances being replicated. A private warning or disgorgement-only penalty would be sufficient. A significant penalty is impossible to reconcile with the finding that the conduct was not deliberate.

(ii) Bearing in mind the penalties imposed in other FSA cases, including that of Mr Osborne[63], the penalty imposed on Mr Einhorn should be much lower. It would be unfair to impose a disproportionate penalty against an individual on the basis that he has accumulated wealth through his hard work over many years.

---

[63] Mr Osborne was fined £350,000 for committing the offence of "improper disclosure" (now "unlawful disclosure" under MAR).

(iii) Any breach was not deliberate or reckless, but totally accidental. If Mr Einhorn had thought he was "anywhere close to the line" he would not have traded. In the circumstances this was, at worst, an understandable misjudgement.

The FSA has found that:

(i) The trading in this case was very significant in terms of volume, highly visible, and related to a large public company. Although the market abuse was inadvertent, it is appropriate and necessary to deter similar errors of judgement in relation to inside information, both in the same circumstances and more generally, through the imposition of a significant penalty.

(ii) Any penalty must be sufficiently substantial to be meaningful, and act as a credible deterrent, to highly visible and influential investors like Mr Einhorn, who have a significant involvement in the markets and commensurate access to company management. Such market participants must act with due caution when liaising with companies and their brokers.

(iii) Mr Einhorn did not act deliberately or recklessly. However, having been asked to and having refused to sign an NDA, with knowledge that the subject of the Punch Call with management and their advisors was the issuance of equity, Mr Einhorn, a highly experienced market professional, should have recognised that there was a real risk of inside information being disclosed to him, and that extreme caution would be required before any trading following the call. His failure to apply the necessary care and rigour, while unintentional, was an extremely serious matter, and warrants a substantial penalty.

Practical "take-aways"

The following pointers – many of which are reinforced elsewhere within this publication – can be taken directly from this case:

- A course of dialogue should be interpreted objectively – in both its entirety and context.
- Company dialogue presents an inherent risk (that inside information might inadvertently be disclosed); and this risk needs to be carefully managed by investor participants.
- Objective substance will prevail over mere disclaimer-type words.
- Inadvertence / innocence / ignorance will not afford a valid defence – there is a clear expectation that investors will apply their own minds and judgement, notwithstanding any assurances or confirmations from others.
- Investors are expected to identify when they have (or might have) received inside information.
- The absence of intent or recklessness does not prevent the commission of the "insider dealing" offence.
- Advice / guidance should be sought, if a "red flag" is identified or there is any question over whether inside information has been divulged – indeed, it is moot whether the FSA would have even pursued the case against Einhorn if he had taken advice at the relevant time.
- Investors cannot reasonably assume that issuers (and their advisers) will not selectively disclose inside information; or that they will duly notify them if they have inadvertently done so.
- The contemporaneous documentation of investment rationale(s) can be helpful – as a timely record of the basis upon which an investment decision was made[64].
- Investors cannot, without more, rely upon the fact that no other participants in a call / meeting considered that inside information had been imparted.

---

[64] See further "Practicalities" chapter.

13
RUMOURS

Context

As highlighted earlier, the dissemination of rumours, where the person who made the dissemination knew, or ought to have known, that the information was false or misleading, is a form of market manipulation. Many firms will have rumour policies, which, amongst other things, cover the creation and communication of, and dealing on the basis of, rumours.

The regulator's view

The regulator has previously defined[65] a "rumour" as "information that is circulated purporting to be fact but which has not yet been verified. A statement is unlikely to be considered a rumour if it is clearly an expression of an individual's or firm's opinion, such as an analyst's view of the prospects of a company".

"The flow of information, when communicated responsibly, is an essential element of efficient markets. Rumours are legitimately circulated through the financial system for a variety of reasons. It is customary for market participants to discuss rumours when accounting for the source of market volatility; when offering an objective assessment of a rumour's likelihood to a client; and when attempting to better understand observable market behaviour.

Nevertheless, **rumours must be handled carefully.** *Their uncontrolled dissemination may lead to rapid and volatile price movements which are unjustified by market fundamentals and undermine general market confidence. Rumours can also be fabricated and spread to manipulate market prices and gain from price movements triggered by them.*

---

[65] Market Watch 30, November 2008.

It is important that regulated firms take this issue seriously. Many firms do this by **drawing clear lines between passing on rumours with appropriate disclaimers and warnings, and the indiscriminate dissemination of unverified and unsubstantiated rumours.** *This is usually done through the formulation of clear and transparent policies on handling rumours and communicating the policies to relevant staff.*"[66] [Our emphasis.]

Case study

Shortly after lunch during a period of financial turbulence, an equity portfolio manager (PM) received a phone call from a broker contact. During this phone call, "hot news" was passed to PM, stating that regulators had requested a named financial institution to cease trading.

Although no reason was given for the alleged regulatory action, PM decided that the news was of sufficient magnitude to send it immediately and without further verification via the Bloomberg messaging system to around 10 – 12 acquaintances. **It was not made clear that this was a rumour that had not been substantiated.** One of the recipients, working at another authorised and large firm (Trader A), decided that such a crucial market-sensitive story should be shared immediately and forwarded the message via Bloomberg's messaging system to approximately 150 of his contacts. As a result, in less than half an hour from the original phone call, the news had reached an employee at the institution the subject of the rumour who immediately alerted his management. Within minutes the regulator was informed and the rumour was retracted by Trader A's firm.

It is clear that these two ill-thought-through decisions by PM and Trader A (together, the **"Individuals"**) could have resulted in massive market-wide repercussions, including substantial disruptions to trade and business of the affected investment bank.

By the end of the day, the regulator had traced the rumour back to its origin and had conducted interviews with all key contributors. The main excuse given by the Individuals was that they "did not stop to think" in

---

[66] Market Watch 30, November 2008.

the thick of trading action and "did not recognise the consequences that their actions could have had" on the market, market participants and, in particular, on the affected financial institution. Neither of them attempted to benefit from the spread of the rumour by taking favourable positions in the institution that was subject to the rumour.

While there appears to have been no intention to disseminate information that was false, the Individuals had a genuine (if arguably naïve) belief that the "rumour" status of the statement was evident when the rumour was passed on. Further, while there was no attempt to profit from the rumour, by virtue of the Individuals passing on the rumour, especially via an information service, **the rumour gained significant credence that was unwarranted considering the source and veracity of the rumour**.

Furthermore, the Individuals had not conducted even simple checks, e.g. they could have checked the regulator's website, any of the regulator's helplines for information, or indeed any of the news agencies for announcements on any regulatory action pertaining to major investment banks. Such verification could have been conducted (i) quickly and (ii) without unduly communicating the rumour to other market participants.

Alternatively, the Individuals could have elevated the matter to their line managers or compliance teams before undertaking any further action. At the bare minimum, the Individuals could have mitigated the damage by ensuring that they clearly stated the information was a rumour and that the information had not (yet) been verified before posting on a message service or loading onto an information service.

Commentary

This case study is based closely upon a scenario previously cited by the regulator as an example of poor practice, likely to warrant enforcement action. It reinforces the need to take the utmost care with the dissemination of rumours – assuming that such practice is permissible under specific internal policies.

14

SUSPICIOUS TRANSACTIONS AND ORDERS

Introduction

Buy-side institutions[67] must establish and maintain effective arrangements, systems and procedures to detect and report suspicious transactions and orders (STORs). Where such a firm has a reasonable suspicion that an order or transaction in any financial instrument, whether placed or executed on or outside a trading venue, could constitute insider dealing, market manipulation or attempted insider dealing or market manipulation, it shall notify the regulator without delay.[68]

Commentary

While the STOR reporting obligation might be regarded as more obviously relevant to sell-side firms – given their sales and trading activities – it nevertheless also applies to the buy-side.

From a buy-side perspective, however, STORs could, for example, stem from: a portfolio manager's order or the communication by a trader / dealer of an order to an external broker or venue. Each of these cases could, in theory at least, arouse suspicion of some form of market abuse. For instance[69], the regulator would expect the dealing function to query any suspicious or anomalous trades to understand the reasoning behind them – for example, a large order to be executed towards the end of a day, on a fund valuation date, which could be an indicator of market manipulation.

---

[67] As well as sell-side firms.
[68] Article 16 of MAR.
[69] And as highlighted in TR 15/1.

The regulator has repeatedly emphasised the importance it attaches to STORs and the expectation on firms to make more STORs than has historically been the case. After all, STORs are arguably the single-best form of intelligence for the regulator in this context.

Indeed, the regulator can, and does, bring enforcement cases (against both firms and individuals) directly related to a failure to recognise and report a suspicious transaction.[70]

Regulatory expectations

The following extracts from a recent FCA speech[71] helpfully outline the regulator's current expectations (and align with the heightened overall focus on non-equity asset classes, as discussed earlier) [our emphasis]:

"The evidence from the STOR submissions we receive is that they are dominated by equity insider dealing, representing well over 70% of all submissions we receive.

There are fewer STOR submissions in equity manipulation than in equity insider dealing, and the number of STORs referencing behaviour in fixed-income and commodity markets is only a small fraction of the total.

Now, without 20:20 vision on the baseline level of market abuse in any market, we can only correlate STORs to outcomes and our own alerting analysis and therefore the FCA would not necessarily assert an implied ratio of STORs between asset classes that we feel will be appropriate. **However, the limited number of non-equity insider dealing STORs does feel like a leading indicator of the capability of the industry to identify potentially manipulative behaviour in equity markets and to monitor and perform surveillance for all types of abuse in fixed-income and commodity markets**.*"*

It is therefore essential that all relevant personnel are familiar with their firm's STOR obligations – **and, importantly, across all applicable asset classes**.

---

[70] For example: *Interactive Brokers (UK) Limited*, 2018; and *Mark Lockwood*, 2009.
[71] Speech by Julia Hoggett, FCA Director of Market Oversight, November 2017.

The STOR regime overlaps, to some degree, with the Suspicious Activity Report regime under money laundering legislation. It is also therefore important to ensure that **both** regimes are taken into consideration, as appropriate.

15

COMMON "BUY-SIDE" ISSUES

Private teams

Some buy-side institutions house "private" teams, which operate within information barriers. These teams are designated "private", due to the fact that they are deemed more likely to become privy to inside information – by virtue of the specifics of their business activities.

In such cases, the firm will typically run two Restricted / Stop Lists – one for the main ("public") side of the business the other for the "private" team(s). This way, the public side will not be unduly fettered, while the private side can go about its business as usual.

It is important that any information barriers employed are routinely monitored for effectiveness; and that relevant personnel are very familiar with these arrangements (including the "dos and the don'ts").

Private assets

Some teams (or "desks") may specialise in direct real asset investments, such as property (real assets). While real assets are not themselves within the scope of MAR, it is still possible that real asset transactions have a MAR angle. For instance:

(1) where the counterparty to a real assets transaction (or its parent) is listed; and the transaction is relatively significant to them (or their parent); and/or

(2) where a firm enters into a joint venture (JV) with a listed partner with a view to entering into a real assets transaction; and the transaction is relatively significant to the JV partner.

In (1), the transaction may constitute inside information in relation to the counterparty (or its parent, as the case may be). In (2), the transaction may constitute inside information in respect of the listed JV partner.

It is therefore essential that those operating in the real assets sphere remain alert to the possibility that they may receive inside information – for example, by virtue of a counterparty's and/or JV partner's (or their respective parent's) listed status. In such cases, relevant Restricted / Stop List entries must be made as per internal policy.

Reliance upon issuer / sell-side assurances

An asset manager and its investment professionals cannot, without more, reasonably rely upon any assurances provided by the issuer or its advisers – for instance, as to whether information is "inside" – **without at the same time also applying its own mind and judgement to the situation**.

Similarly, it cannot be reasonably assumed that anything and everything disclosed by a listed issuer or its advisers must, by definition, not be inside information – as otherwise this would amount to "unlawful disclosure". In other words, reliance cannot be placed on the premise that an issuer (or its advisers) will at all times act in accordance with MAR and not commit any MAR offences. While, of course, this should always (ideally, at least) be the case, a buy-side investor cannot assume as much; and must again apply its own judgement.

Inadvertent wall-crossings

One of the most frustrating situations for an investment manager is an inadvertent wall-crossing – where a party is made "inside" without its prior agreement.

What can we do about it?

This will very much depend upon the particular situation.

In some cases, the buy-side firm's Compliance department will contact its counterpart at the sell-side institution to voice its concerns and to seek some form of satisfactory resolution. However, this will entirely depend on the specific facts and/or the views of the sell-side firm.

While there may not be a technical regulatory notification obligation upon the buy-side firm in these circumstances, it is always open to the investment manager's Compliance department to voice any concerns with the regulator.

Based on experience, it would be unusual for the issuer (or its sell-side advisers) to agree to "cleanse" the information (by making a public announcement). Indeed, this is often because the issuer disagrees that the information was "inside". Such a stance is not especially surprising, given that a concession (that inside information was disclosed) would arguably be tantamount to an admission to the "unlawful disclosure" offence.

Can we self-cleanse?

Where the issuer is (for whatever reason) unwilling to make any cleansing announcement, a buy-side firm may occasionally feel as though it has little choice, in the circumstances (particularly, if time is of the essence), in making its own public announcement of the relevant information – with the intention of thereby cleansing itself of its insider status. While there are a few recent instances of such a measure being taken by an asset manager, these involved exceptional time-critical "distressed" circumstances.

As a general matter, the regulator would much prefer that any inside information sourced from an issuer is announced by *that issuer* – and not, for example, by a disgruntled third party that would be seen as effectively having taken matters into its own hands. This will help serve to ensure that the dissemination of inside information is controlled and orderly.

Any firm intending to self-cleanse in this way should first seek advice.

16
PRACTICALITIES

This chapter contains a miscellany of practical insights, pointers and "war-stories" – all of which have direct relevance to the "buy-side".

Use of Restricted / Stop Lists

Most, if not all, asset managers maintain Restricted / Stop Lists, which typically operate a "one-in-all-in" model. Whenever any inside information is received within the firm, it must be promptly logged on the Restricted / Stop List; whereupon all dealing in the relevant security (both for funds and on personal account) is prohibited[72]. Accordingly, all personnel within the firm are *deemed* – for these purposes at least[73] – to be inside.

A key rationale behind the "one-in-all-in" model is to preclude any dealing by, attributable to, or on behalf of, the firm whilst it is in possession of inside information – in which case, as explained in chapter 6, the firm would be presumed to have insider dealt. In essence, therefore, the "one-in-all-in" model is a cautionary measure.

On occasion, however, the operation of this model can lead to a tension. By way of example, a portfolio manager (PM) places an order, only to discover that this order has been blocked by the order management system because someone else within the firm is "inside" on the relevant stock (with the stock therefore featuring on the Restricted / Stop List). In such a scenario, PM may well feel frustrated that he cannot effect a transaction in which he has a strong conviction and which, in his view, would be in his fund's investors' best interests.

---

[72] For so long as that issuer / security remains on the Restricted / Stop List.
[73] See further chapter 7.

Practicalities

There is no magic solution to this particular conundrum. However, it is generally accepted that, in such (limited) circumstances, *legitimate* market abuse risk management considerations can prevail over the duty to act in clients' best interests.

It is correspondingly important that Restricted / Stop Lists are kept up to date and do not contain stale or otherwise unnecessary entries. Otherwise, firms would be exposed to the challenge – whether from a regulator and/or a disgruntled investor – that they were **unduly** restricting investment activity (contrary to their clients' best interests obligation), through the continued presence of such redundant entries on the Restricted / Stop List.

"Abundance of caution" entries

In certain circumstances, firms may opt to record an entry on the Restricted List out of an abundance of caution – in particular, where it is unclear as to whether or not they have actually received "inside information". In any such cases, it is advisable to include a note within the relevant Restricted / Stop List entry, indicating that it was made "out of an abundance of caution" – so that it can be readily distinguished from a "normal" entry. This can prove helpful if it is subsequently decided to "override" the restriction, following a further, more detailed analysis which concluded that the information was not inside. In other words, it would make the override easier to explain, if ever subsequently challenged.

Some firms have been known to use this technique as a quasi-Watch List. In this way, any Restricted / Stop List entry marked "abundance of caution" would cause a *prima facie* block – but one which could potentially be overridden by Compliance – if deemed appropriate on the particular facts.

Awkward questions

"War story"

A portfolio manager (PM) has been wall-crossed, following a market sounding (relating to a proposed imminent equity placing by Company X). While "inside", PM receives a Bloomberg message from a third-party broker, enquiring as to whether PM *"had heard the market rumour that Company X would soon be tapping the market"* (not necessarily realising that PM was in fact "inside").

▸ How should PM respond?

Ideally, PM would either completely ignore or plead ignorance to this enquiry.

In a recent (non-published) case, with almost identical facts, the portfolio manager concerned saw fit to respond to the broker as follows: ";-)" – yes, with a wink sign! Needless to say, this act was viewed extremely dimly by his firm and the regulator, and the individual was severely disciplined.

While any such situations may in practice be rare, it is nevertheless vitally important that insiders on the receiving end of similar enquiries behave appropriately; and do not directly or indirectly disclose any inside information with which they have been entrusted.

Inadvertent disclosure / receipt of inside information

No firm is perfect, and mistakes will inevitably occur, from time to time. For instance, investment managers may, on occasion, either inadvertently disclose or receive inside information. In any such case, it is crucial that the issue is escalated as soon as possible (ideally, to Legal or Compliance, in the first instance), with a view to minimising and containing any damage. **Time will often be of the essence.**

In the case of inadvertent receipt, it is paramount that the sensitive information is not forwarded on to others by the initial recipient – save where expressly authorised to do so by Legal or Compliance. In essence, this is little more than an application of the important "need-to-know" principle, discussed later in this chapter.

"War story"

An investment professional (IP) received a highly price-sensitive email in error from an investment bank. IP finds this so amusing that he forwards the relevant email on to his entire team (globally), accompanied by a smiley face emoticon!

Practicalities

Indeed, IP made matters even worse by accessing (and even printing off) the various attachments to the email.

Needless to say, IP was disciplined for his inappropriate actions, receiving a final written warning and a significant bonus reduction. IP should have appreciated that he would be expected, in such circumstances, to keep the email strictly contained (and confined to his inbox) – unless instructed otherwise by Legal or Compliance.

Need-to-know

Most, if not all, investment managers will operate a "need-to-know" policy – pursuant to which inside information may only ever be shared on a strict need-to-know basis[74].

Some firms will monitor this policy by maintaining an "insider list", comprising those individuals who are actually in possession of the inside information (together with the date and time that they became insiders). As discussed earlier, this is entirely distinct from the *deeming* of all personnel to be inside under the "one-in-all-in" model.

The FCA has made a number of observations in this context, and this **remains an area of concerted regulatory focus**:

"Good practice

One firm we visited kept a detailed log of who knew inside information. Knowledge of the information was not shared beyond the person wall-crossed, other team members who needed the information to fulfil professional responsibilities (e.g. a fund manager who might participate in a proposed placing), and compliance. Senior management and traders were unaware of the information or the restriction, unless they attempted to trade the stock. Even then they were only informed of the restriction, rather than receiving the inside information. Limiting the sharing of inside information to those who need to know is appropriate and the documentation of who knows what is one way of monitoring whether this policy is working effectively.

---

[74] Alongside the requirement that any such disclosure must also be in the normal exercise of an employment, profession or duties – see further chapter 7.

Poor practice
One firm notified all traders when inside information had been received as an interim control to prevent trading until a system block was in place (we consider system blocks and pre-trade controls in more detail below). In addition to being notified of the company name, the traders also received the detail of the inside information. This unnecessary dissemination of inside information was contrary to the firm's need-to-know policy and increased the risk of market abuse."[75]

Documenting investment rationale(s)

Several asset managers require (or, alternatively) encourage the documentation of investment rationale(s) by the relevant portfolio manager. Such practice can be helpful in, amongst other things, monitoring investment decision-making and enabling more effective post-trade surveillance or enquiries. Contemporaneously documented investment rationale(s) could also serve as an invaluable "defence" (or rebuttal) to an allegation that a person "used" inside information (and therefore "insider dealt").

For instance, a portfolio manager (PM) returns from a meeting with Company Y and immediately places an order to divest his fund's entire holding of Company Y stock. This scenario could, on its face, be viewed as suspicious – namely, one interpretation is that PM dealt having just received negative inside information at the meeting. While every situation will be highly fact-specific, it might just be that PM's documented investment rationale(s) – namely, his loss of faith in the credibility of management, based on their perceived poor performance at the meeting – could help to rebut any charge that PM insider dealt.

Clearly, as with any situation in which contemporaneous notes are made, it is important to ensure that the record represents an accurate and unambiguous depiction.

Verbal orders
Many firms will allow for verbal orders in exceptional cases – most obviously, where the investment professional concerned has no access

---

[75] TR 15/1 "Asset Management Firms and the Risk of Market Abuse", 2015.

Practicalities

to any of the "normal" modes of communicating an order, and time is of the essence.

In any such circumstance, it is important that the investment professional promptly follows up by ensuring that his order is appropriately documented, including, where required, his investment rationale(s) – as soon as he had access to the appropriate system.

Training

While there is no strict requirement as to the mode and frequency of market conduct training, there has been a discernible trend of late for firms to utilise a combination of tailored computer-based and interactive face-to-face training. Computer-based training is typically rolled-out annually. Supplemental "in-person" training will often take place every one or two years.

Some firms will require all employees to attend; whereas others adopt a risk-based approach by focussing their efforts on investment professionals.

It is self-evidently essential that all training is appropriately tailored and relevant to the particular audience. Case studies and "real-life" scenarios can be particularly effective in achieving full audience engagement. The value of affording attendees the opportunity to ask questions and challenge cannot be understated.

As emphasised earlier, a **consistently high state of intuitive awareness across staff is paramount**. High-quality training sessions are the single best means of reinforcing such awareness – to ensure that all relevant personnel are "kept on their toes" and remain vigilant.

"Expert networks"

Several investment managers utilise the services of specialist external consultants (or "expert networks") to help inform their investment theses. While this is a perfectly acceptable practice *per se*, it is important that the inherent risks are appropriately managed. Safeguards employed by users of expert networks will often include, amongst other things, contractual representations from the consultant, confirming that: (i) none of its employees have recently (say within the past six to nine months) worked for any "target" company; (ii) none of its employees are privy to any inside information on any target company; and, in any event, (iii) the consultant will not disclose any inside information.

Additionally, some firms will require the key topics discussed at any meetings with consultants to be documented.

If, during the course of the engagement of an external consultant, any doubt arises as to the status or provenance of particular information[76], this should be escalated to Legal or Compliance.

Can one portfolio manager within a firm deal (say, acquire) in a particular stock in the knowledge that another portfolio manager within the same firm has just placed a significant (and likely market-moving) (buy) trade in the same stock (and that trade has not yet been reported to the market)?

On one (admittedly rather technical) view, a person (here, the firm) cannot be "inside" on its own trading activities; and, therefore, the answer to this question would be "no".

However, and putting aside any technical arguments, it is certainly doubtful whether the regulator would concur with this stance[77]. Whether or not this was an actionable case of "insider trading", there is a real risk that this would in any event be seen to offend against certain of the overarching principles with which firms must comply – most obviously, acting with integrity and observing proper standards of market conduct.

---

[76] For instance, if information appears so specific so as to signal that it might actually be inside information.
[77] As evidenced in TR 15/1, in which the FCA indicated that this would be regarded as problematic.

17
SCENARIOS

Scenario 1

A portfolio manager (PM) agrees to be "wall-crossed" in the context of a pre-sounding exercise being conducted by Broker Ltd on behalf of XYZ Plc (a listed property company, which is seeking a joint venture partner for a major imminent property acquisition). Prior to the disclosure of any inside information, Broker Ltd assures PM that he is "only likely to be restricted for a maximum of two weeks".

Three weeks pass, with no contact from Broker Ltd (and no announcement by XYZ). PM contacts Broker Ltd to enquire as to the status of the contemplated transaction. In response, PM's contact at Broker Ltd confirms that the proposed transaction has been "put on ice for the time being".

▸ Where exactly does this leave PM?

Commentary

The response (that the transaction has been "put on ice for the time being") is unhelpful; and PM has been left in a real predicament. It would therefore be advisable for PM to continue to regard himself as "inside", pending either: (a) a satisfactory (i.e. clearer) subsequent confirmation that, for example, the transaction was no longer under consideration; or (b) the passage of an appropriate length of time (deemed sufficiently long for the prospect of the originally envisaged transaction to have become so uncertain – whether due to the effluxion of time and/or possibly other variables).

Put another way, PM would be running a significant risk of subsequent challenge if he relied, without more, on the contact's response as an effective cleansing.

Scenarios

Scenario 2

Q Plc (in which one of your funds is a 5% bondholder) is about to announce a significant acquisition, which will require bondholder support. You have just been (consensually) wall-crossed by an investment bank acting on behalf of Q Plc, with a view to gauging your attitude towards the prospective transaction. During the dialogue with the investment bank, you are provided with an indication as to Q's current trading performance (which, incidentally, you didn't consider necessary for the purposes of the pre-sounding).

You promptly log Q's bonds on the Restricted / Stop List.

The transaction is announced to the market 48 hours later.

You contact Compliance to request immediate removal of Q from the Restricted / Stop List.

▶ Have you acted appropriately here?

Commentary

Before requesting the removal of Q from the Restricted / Stop List, you should first have considered whether the information relating to Q's current trading performance has also been "cleansed". If not, Q should remain on the Restricted / Stock List.

It is important to read and digest the full contents of an announcement – to check and confirm whether it cleanses **all** inside information in your possession. This should not simply be assumed.

Scenario 3

You are accidentally sent a sensitive email (marked "strictly confidential") by a corporate financier friend. The email reveals that Y plc, a large listed potash company, is being investigated by the environmental authorities.

There are three listed potash companies.

▶ What do you do?

Commentary

You will need to log Y Plc on the Restricted / Stop List. Given the small size of the listed potash sector, you should also, however, consider whether the information also constitutes "inside information" on the other two listed potash companies. If so, they too should be entered onto the Restricted / Stop List.

This is an example of a potential read-across scenario highlighted earlier (and repeated below).

"Read-across" scenarios

Issuers

It is possible[78] that, in certain circumstances, inside information relating to one company (A) may also constitute inside information in relation to another company (B). This will always be a very fact-specific determination; and will likely depend upon a number of factors, including (but not limited to):

- The nature / import of the inside information itself – for example, whether it is very specific to Company A and therefore unlikely to have any material implications for company B / the wider sector.
- Whether A and B operate in the same industry / sector; and share similar characteristics (e.g. customer-base, products, technologies, locations, regulatory environments, financial

---

[78] Albeit, this will be more the exception, rather than the norm.

Scenarios

conditions, etc), which, in the circumstances, increase the likelihood of Company B also being affected by the inside information.
- If so, the number of other listed issuers within the same industry / sector.
- The relative significance of Company A in the context of the wider listed sector / industry as a whole. For instance, is Company A a relative minnow?

Scenario 4

A fund manager (FM) commissions a report from an external consultant who specialises in the technology sector. FM is particularly interested to learn whether there may be any undervalued technology companies in which one of her funds might invest (as it is "underweight" in that sector).

FM receives the consultant's report, which makes for interesting reading. FM is surprised by the specificity of certain information contained in the report (relating to PharmCom Inc, a US-listed company). On reflection, she is struggling to see how this information can have been obtained other than from an inside source at PharmaCom.

▸ Where does this leave FM?

Commentary

FM should discuss her concerns with Legal and/or Compliance at the earliest opportunity. If, following such discussions, it is concluded (on balance) that inside information has been received, PharmCom Inc. should be added to the Restricted / Stop List.

It would also be advisable for FM's firm to review its controls around the engagement of external consultants – as this incident may be taken to indicate that such controls are not sufficiently effective.

Scenarios

Scenario 5

A portfolio manager (PM) is intending to place a large "buy" order (the "Order") in stock X. This is very likely to result in an increase in the price of X shares and in the prices of the shares of other companies in the same sector (as it will be perceived as a generally positive sector development). Immediately ahead of placing the Order, and in anticipation of such upwards share movements, PM also places "buy" orders in certain other companies in X's sector (the "Other Orders").

At a recent training session, PM was told that "you cannot be inside on your own trading activities". On this basis, PM believes that he was entitled to act as he did.

▸ Has PM done anything wrong?

Commentary

The Other Orders [placed by PM ahead of the X Order] would be vulnerable to regulatory challenge. MAR states that [our emphasis]:

*"... the mere fact that a person uses its own knowledge that it has decided to acquire or dispose of financial instruments in the acquisition or disposal of **those** financial instruments shall not of itself constitute use of inside information."*[79]

PM has inside information on X – namely, the knowledge of his impending Order in X. On the basis of the above extract, he is entitled to use that information to acquire X shares.

However, this does not necessarily mean that he can use that inside information to acquire **other** shares, which are, to some degree at least, correlated to X. On one view, this could be construed as insider dealing – in financial instruments "the price of value of which depends on or has an effect on the price of" X[80]. Alternatively, and in any event, it is likely to be considered as a breach of the principles – whether acting with integrity and/or observing proper standards of market conduct.

---

[79] Article 9.5 of MAR.
[80] Article 2.1(d) of MAR.

Scenario 6

Following a market sounding exercise, a fund manager (FM) is an insider on ZCorp Inc., a company listed on both US and UK markets. FM knows that ZCorp is about to announce a significant disposal of a loss-making unit.

FM goes to the bookmakers and places a fixed-odds bet that, at the end of the month, the share price of ZCorp will have risen by at least 5%.

- Has PM done anything wrong?

Commentary

While there may be a technical argument that FM's fixed-odds bet does not itself constitute a "financial instrument" (under MAR) — although this is far from clear — FM would in any event be exposed to a charge[81] of failing to act with integrity and/or to observe proper standards of market conduct. Indeed, this is potentially exacerbated by the fact that FM has seemingly attempted to (cynically) circumvent the market conduct regime.

---

[81] Under the Principles.

Scenario 7

A portfolio manager (PM) receives a call from Tarquin, a bulge-bracket investment banker. Tarquin wants to *"sound out"* PM *"about an interesting opportunity that may arise in relation to a large European company"*. PM asks for some further colour, but stresses that he does not, at this stage, wish to be wall-crossed by receiving any inside information.

Tarquin proceeds to tell PM that the opportunity relates to a listed Scandinavian pharmaceuticals company; and that time is very much of the essence.

PM responds by telling Tarquin that he thinks Tarquin may have over-stepped the mark and disclosed inside information. Tarquin disagrees and is adamant that he has not wall-crossed PM.

- Is PM right? What considerations will be relevant?
- What should PM do?
- Has PM done anything wrong?
- To what extent can PM rely upon Tarquin's assertions?

Commentary

PM obviously feels that he has received sufficient information to enable him to identify the company concerned – and he should follow his instinct. PM cannot blindly rely on Tarquin's assertions.

PM should discuss this scenario with Legal or Compliance; following which, if the consensus view is that PM is inside, the relevant issuer should promptly be added to the Restricted / Stop List.

Scenario 8

Your firm has entered into a joint venture arrangement with a partner firm (P) – with a view to a prospective infrastructure debt transaction. P is a private company with listed debt; and also a subsidiary of a listed company.

▶ What market conduct-related issues does this scenario present?

Commentary

Consideration will need to be given as to whether your firm is now "inside" on P and/or P's listed parent. This will likely depend on the relative significance of the proposed joint venture to P and to P's parent. If it is ultimately determined that the proposed transaction would constitute information that a reasonable investor in P / P's parent would be likely to use as part of the basis of his or her investment decisions, then P / P's parent (as appropriate) should be logged on the firm's Restricted / Stop List.

Scenarios

Scenario 9

Your firm is (to your knowledge) about to bring an action against C Bank plc in respect of an allegedly misleading rights issue prospectus issued by C Bank. Proceedings are to be served over the next few weeks. Your fund holds a significant stake in C Bank.

You receive a compelling internal research paper suggesting that C Bank is overvalued and recommending an immediate "scaling back" of your position.

▸ Are you free to follow through on the analyst's recommendation?

Commentary

It might prudently be assumed that the knowledge of the impending litigation against C Bank is negative "inside information", which, once announced, would result in a C Bank share price drop.

While any immediate sale might, *in reality*, be driven by the bearish research paper, this would likely be very difficult to demonstrate, if ever challenged. As a matter of law, it would be assumed that your dealing was, in part at least, influenced by the knowledge of the impending litigation. Rebutting that assumption may prove extremely difficult in practice – in essence, this would involve persuading the regulator that the inside information played no role in your divestment decision. While clearly helpful, the internal research paper may well not itself suffice.

This scenario serves to highlight the importance of applying a practical "overlay" to any technical legal arguments.

INDEX

A

Alternative Investment Management Association (AIMA) 63

B

BCI 61-63
big-boy letters 62, 63
Borrower Confidential Information, see BCI
Brexit..................................... 11, 29

C

civil regime 11, 13-14
cleanse 10, 95, 106
commodity markets 90
company meetings / dialogue 65-67
Compliance team .... 25, 58, 71, ... 80-81, 87, 94-95, ... 98-100, 103, 106, 109, 112
contract for difference 24
Criminal Justice Act 1993, Section 53(1) 13
criminal regime 11, 13-14

D

disclosing market participant, see DMP
disclosure
 improper 44, 81
 unlawful .... 12 ,13, 27, 38, 43, ... 45, 54, 57, 81, 84, 95
DMP – disclosing market participant 15, 54
documenting investment rationale 101

E

David Einhorn 24, 37, 69-83
Einhorn / Greenlight .... 12, 24, ... 32, 53, 59, 66, 69-83
ESMA 15, 24
EU 9, 11, 21, 23-24
European Securities and Markets Authority, see ESMA
expert networks 102

115

F

FCA 15, 25, 29, 33, 44,
.... 51, 70, 90, 100, 103
Principles 15
Director of Market Oversight
.... 25, 33, 90
Financial Conduct Authority,
see FCA
financial instruments ... 17, 21-24,
.... 27-28, 31, 33-34, 35-36,
.... 48, 50, 54, 56, 106
Financial Services Authority,
see FSA
fixed-income markets 90
FSA 41, 70, 71, 75-83
FTSE 24
Fundamental Principles
.... 14, 16, 17-19, 25, 47, 64

G

Greenlight,
see *Einhorn / Greenlight*

H

Hoggett, Julia 25, 33, 90

I

illustrative example 24, 29
improper disclosure 44, 81
inadvertent disclosure 67, 99
inadvertent wall-crossing
.... 10, 94
initial public offering, see IPO

Inside Information
definition 27
illustrative example 29
non-issuer originated 40
non-public 28-29, 40
precise nature 27
source / origin 32
insider dealing 12, 35-41
attempting 35
inducing and recommending
.... 35
non-issuer originated 40
offences 35
rebuttable presumption 36
intention to float 58
Interactive Brokers (UK) Limited
.... 90
internal research paper 114
investment rationale
.... 83, 101-102
IPO 58
issuer / sell-side assurances ... 94
issuers 27, 31-33, 40, 94,

J

joint venture 93, 105, 113
Julia Hoggett 25, 33, 90

K

Kyprios 16, 64

L

Lafonta v AMF 28
Loan Market Association (LMA) 61-64
Loans and other 'out-of-scope' instruments 61, 62, 63, 64
Lockwood, Mark 90

M

MAR – Market Abuse Regulation
 Annex 1 48
 Article 2.1(d) 110
 Article 2.4 23
 Article 7.1(a) 27
 Article 7.2 28
 Article 7.4 30
 Article 8 57
 Article 8.1 35
 Article 8(2) 35
 Article 9.5 110
 Article 10 .... 43, 57
 Article 11.3 54
 Article 11.4 54
 Article 11.5 54
 Article 12 48
 Article 13 48
 Article 14 43
 Articles 14(b) 35
 Article 16 89
 Article 123 80-81
 Recital (23) 40
 Recital (24) 36, 40
 Recital (26) 36

sanctions 14, 16, 24
scope .... 12, 16, 21-25, ... 33, 36, 64, 93
territorial reach / application 12, 21-25
Mark Lockwood 90
market abuse ...... 11, 13, 17, 25, 27, ... 33, 35, 37, 38, 44, 47, 65, ... 70-71, 80-82, 89-90, 98, 101
Market Abuse Regulation, see MAR
market manipulation 12, 13, 18, 25, 47-51, 85, 89
market sounding recipient, see MSR
market soundings 10, 53-59
 defined 53
 DMP requirements 54
 gauging the interest of potential investors 58
 MSR requirements 56
 prior to the announcement . 58
 process 54
Merrill Lynch International (MLI) 69-70, 72
MNPI, also see inside information 27
Morton and Parry 41
MSR 54-56
MTF – multilateral trading facility 21-23

117

N

NDA 69, 74-77, 80, 82
Nicholas Kyprios 16, 64
non-disclosure agreement,
 see NDA
non-discretionary rules 23
non-equity asset classes ... 25, 90
non-public information
 .... 28-29, 40

O

Offences 10, 12, 13, 17-18,
 .... 47-48, 51, 94
 insider dealing 12, 35-41
 market manipulation 12, 13,
  .... 18, 25, 47-51, 85, 89
one-in-all-in model
 .... 37-38, 97, 100
organised trading facility,
 see OTF
Andrew Osborne 72-74, 81
OTF – organised trading facility
 21-23

P

Parry (*Morton* and *Parry*) 41
pre-sounding exercise 105
precise nature 27, 33
private teams 93
private assets 93
proper standards of market
 conduct 15-16, 45,
  .... 64, 103, 110, 111
public censure 14, 16

public domain 10, 28, 30
Punch Taverns Plc 24, 69-83

R

read-across scenarios 32, 107
reasonable investor
 .... 10, 30-31, 67, 76-77, 113
reasonable investor test 10
regulated market 21-23
Regulatory Technical Standards,
 see RTS
Restricted / Stop Lists
 .... 93, 97-98
 abundance of caution entries
  98
 use of 97
RTS 15, 54-55
rumours 12, 45, 48, 66,
 .... 85-87, 99

S

sanctions 10, 14, 16, 24
 prohibitions 14, 16, 17-18,
  .... 23, 57
 public censure 14, 16
 unlimited fines 14, 16
SCI – Syndicate Confidential
 Information 61-63
sell-side assurances 94
Stop Lists 93, 97-98
STORs – suspicious transactions
 and orders 12, 89-91
suspicious transactions and
 orders, see STORs ....

Syndicate Confidential
   Information, see SCI ....

T

trade................. 10, 21-24, 38-40,
   ....48-49, 51, 61-63, 70-71,
   ..... 78-80, 86, 89, 100-101, 103
trading venue .. 21, 23, 49-50, 89
training 57, 102, 110

U

unfair advantage 17-18, 40, 43
unlawful disclosure 12, 13,
   .... 27, 38, 43-46,
   .... 54, 57, 81, 84, 95
   encouraging or inducing 45
   the offence 12, 13, 27, 38, 43,
      .... 45, 54, 57, 81, 94-95
unlimited fines.................... 14, 16
verbal orders........................... 101

W

wall-crossing 45, 53, 59,
   .... 69-73, 75, 80,
   .... 94, 98, 105, 106, 112
   inadvertent..................... 10, 94
Walter 51